JLA
図書館実践シリーズ 48

図書館員のための英会話ハンドブック 国内編

改訂版

日本図書館協会出版委員会 編

日本図書館協会

Librarian's Handbook of English Communication on Everyday Library Activities in Japan, Revised Edition

(JLA Monograph Series for Library Practitioners ; 48)

図書館員のための英会話ハンドブック : 国内編 / 日本図書館協会出版
委員会編
改訂版
東京 : 日本図書館協会, 2024
x, 153 p ; 19 cm
(JLA 図書館実践シリーズ ; 48)
ISBN 978-4-8204-2408-6

機器種別: 機器不用
キャリア種別: 冊子
表現種別: テキスト
表現形の言語: 日本語
著作の優先タイトル: 図書館員のための英会話ハンドブック　国内編
改訂版||トショカンイン ノ タメ ノ エイカイワ ハンドブック コクナイ
ヘン カイテイバン
創作者: 日本図書館協会出版委員会||ニホン トショカン キョウカイ
シュッパン イインカイ
BSH4: 英語－会話
NDC10: 837.8

まえがき

　本書は，1996 年 9 月に日本図書館協会より出版された『図書館員のための英会話ハンドブック　国内編』の改訂版です。

　想定する読者層は公共・大学・専門図書館等の利用者対応をする図書館員で，英語力は初・中級向けとし，外国人への応対で日常遭遇する場面，状況別の基本的な言い回しを盛り込んだ本です。

　図書館の利用者も外国人が増えていく中，出版以降多くの図書館員等に活用いただき，おかげさまで増刷を繰り返してまいりました。

　しかし，図書館サービスの変化や電子媒体の普及に伴い，1996 年刊行当時の図書館用語やフレーズが，現代のサービスに合っていない部分も多く見られるようになりました。

　近年，日本図書館協会では，2023 年 11 月に『図書館員のための「やさしい日本語」』（JLA Booklet no.15）を出版するなど，外国人利用者に対応する図書館員向けの本も出版してまいりましたが，本書の改訂を望む声も多くいただいておりました。

　そこでこのたび，初版発行から約 30 年の時を経て，改訂版を発行する運びとなりました。内容は，基本的に初版をベースとしました。Ⅰ．カウンターやフロアでの簡単な案内，Ⅱ．電話による問い合わせ，Ⅲ．貸出・返却，Ⅳ．図書館間相互貸借，Ⅴ．レファレンスサービス，Ⅵ．館内案内，付録として寄贈等に係るメール等の例文，英文利用案内，索引という構成です。

OPAC やデータベース，電子ジャーナルといったように，現代に合った内容になるよう例文を修正・追記しました。加えて，初版にはなかった地震・火災等の「非常時」の項目を新たに設けました。

最近は，Web 上での翻訳ツール等も充実し，精度も日々向上しています。このような便利なツールも有効に活用しつつ，本書が図書館員の皆様の「困ったときの力強い助っ人」となれば幸いです。

2024 年 10 月

日本図書館協会出版委員会委員　槇盛可那子

目 次

まえがき　　iii

Ⅰ　カウンターやフロアでの簡単な案内 ……… 1

入館手続き ……… 2

入館に手続きが必要な場合　　2

学内利用者に対する規則　　3

荷物の持ち込み　　4

ロッカーの利用　　5

施設案内 ……… 7

蔵書構成案内　　7

フロア案内　　8

〈比較的小さな図書館で案内図のある場合〉　　8

〈大きな図書館や，建物が2つ以上ある図書館〉　　9

施設の利用と予約　　11

資料別案内 ……… 14

単行本，雑誌，新聞，他資料の配架場所　　14

各種サービス ……… 21

複写　　21

マイクロフィルムの複写　　25

コピー機のトラブル　　26

購入希望　　26

目次………v

目 次

障害者サービス　29
団体貸出　29

退館 30
入退館ゲートが鳴ったら　30

非常時 32
地震が発生したら　32
火災が発生したら　32

Ⅱ　電話による問い合わせ 35

電話を取ったらあわてずに 36
利用資格の確認 37
利用資格に制限がない場合（公共図書館等）　37
利用資格に制限がある場合（大学・専門図書館等）　37

交通機関・経路 39
開館のお知らせ 41
開館時間　41
休館・閉館　42

訪問の約束 45
移動図書館の巡回スポット 47

contents

忘れ物 ·· 49

Ⅲ　貸出・返却 ·································· 51

登録 ·· 52
公共図書館　52
大学図書館　54
図書館利用者カードに関する取扱いについて　55

貸出規則 ·· 57
禁帯出資料　57
貸出期間・貸出冊数　58
罰則，延滞料　59

資料請求，館内利用 ························ 61

貸出 ·· 63
カウンターでの手続き　63
自動貸出機　64

返却 ·· 66

予約 ·· 69
書架にない場合　69
電話で連絡　71

目次········vii

目 次

貸出期間延長 ………………………………………………… 72
紛失 ………………………………………………………… 74
督促 ………………………………………………………… 76

Ⅳ 図書館間相互貸借 ……………… 77

図書 ………………………………………………………… 78
雑誌論文 …………………………………………………… 81
海外 ILL の利用 …………………………………………… 83

Ⅴ レファレンスサービス ……… 85

所蔵調査 …………………………………………………… 86
　電話での応答　　86
　カウンターで　　90

所在調査 …………………………………………………… 93
事項調査 …………………………………………………… 97
利用案内 …………………………………………………… 99
　単行本の分類法　　99
　OPAC の利用方法　　101

viii

contents

《質問例　図書の検索》　103

《質問例　OPAC 件名》　105

レファレンスブック案内　105

《質問例　人物情報》　106

《質問例　団体情報》　107

《質問例　統計》　108

他館の紹介　109

オンラインリソース 112

国立国会図書館デジタル化資料送信サービス　112

データベース，電子ジャーナルなど　112

《質問例　電子ジャーナル》　114

SDI サービス　116

検索講習会　117

《質問例　インターネット》　117

研究者向けサービス 119

雑誌の投稿規定　119

特許情報調査　119

VI　館内案内 121

サイン，各種表示，催し物案内 122

館内放送 124

目次………ix

目 次

付録 127

1. 寄贈 128

- （1）寄贈依頼のサンプル　128
- （2）雑誌の寄贈依頼の簡単なサンプル　129
- （3）日本語・英語兼用の受領書　130
- （4）交換依頼とその礼状　130
- （5）住所変更　131
- （6）宛名訂正　132

2. クレーム処理 132

3. 国立国会図書館東京本館　利用案内 「Quick guide」 135

入館　135

図書館に持ち込めないもの　138

退館　139

忘れ物　139

4. 国立国会図書館国際子ども図書館　利用案内 140

小さなお子様連れの方へ　140

おむつ替え等に利用できるベビーシート　140

授乳スペース　141

食事スペース　141

トイレ　142

あとがき　143

事項索引　145

x

Ⅰ

カウンターや フロアでの簡単な案内

**Basic assistance at the counter
or on the floor**

入館手続き　Admission to the building

◆**入館に手続きが必要な場合**　**For institutions such as university libraries that are restricted to qualified users**

User（U）：○○大学の教員ですが，手続きが必要ですか？

I teach at ○○ University. Are there any necessary procedures?

U：私は○○大学の学生ですが，手続きが必要ですか？

I am a student at ○○ University. Are there any necessary procedures?

Librarian（L）：紹介状をお持ちですか？

Do you have a letter of introduction?

U：これでよろしいでしょうか。

Is this all right?

L：わかりました。それではこの学外利用者の用紙に記入してください。

Fine. Please complete this visitor form.

ここにお名前，ここには所属を記入してください。

Insert your name and affiliation here.

U：紹介状はありません。

I don't have a letter of introduction.

L：申し訳ございませんが，紹介状のない学外の方の利用はできません。

I'm sorry, but without a letter of introduction, you can't use the library.

L：身分証明書をお持ちでしたら，提示してください。利用できます。

> I need to see some personal identification. Fine. You can use the library.

身分証がなければ，入館することができません。

> You can't enter the library without identification.

L：手続きは終わりました。

> That's all for the application.

この入館カードを首からかけて見えるようにしてご利用ください。

> Please wear this admission card around your neck so that it is visible during your visit.

このバッジをつけてください。

> Please put on this badge.

ゲートを開けますので，ここからお入りください。

> Please enter through the gate, as it is now open.

お帰りの際はバッジをこちらに返却してください。

> Please return your badge when you leave.

◆学内利用者に対する規則　　**Rules for users affiliated with the institution**

Librarian（L）：入館ゲートで図書館利用者カード（学生証／職員証／ ID カード）をリーダーにタッチさせて入館ゲートを通ってください。

> Please pass through the gate by simply holding your library card（student ID/staff ID/ID card）over the card reader.

入館手続き………3

無効なカードではゲートを通れません。

If the card is invalid, then the user can't pass through the gate.

L：規則により図書館利用者カードを忘れると入館できません。

According to the rules, if you forget your library card, you can't enter the library.

L：この大学の所属であることを証明するものを他にお持ちですか？　学生証か，身分証明証をお持ちください。臨時のカードを発行します。

Do you have anything else to indicate that you are affiliated with the university? Student identification card or other identification? We issue a temporary card.

◆荷物の持ち込み　　**Bringing things into the library**

User（U）：荷物はどうしたらよいでしょう？

What should I do with my belongings?

Librarian（L）：そのままお持ちください。

Simply take them with you.

L：それは持ち込めません。荷物はお預かりします。

They can't be taken inside. Leave them here.

L：荷物は預かることはできません。

I can't hold them for you.

L：こちらにお戻りになるまでお預かりします。

I'll hold them for you until you return.

U：傘は持ち込めますか？

May I take my umbrella inside?

L：濡れた傘は，入口ホールにある傘立てに入れるか，備え付けのビニール袋をご利用ください。視聴覚室に入るときはビニール袋に入っていても傘は持ち込めません。

> If it is wet, leave it in the umbrella stand in the entrance hall or place it in one of the plastic bags provided. But you can't take a wet umbrella into the audio-visual room even if it is placed in a plastic bag.

L：ロッカーがありますので，荷物はロッカーに入れてください。

> There are lockers. Please place your belongings in a locker.

貴重品は身につけてお持ちください。

> Keep your valuables with you.

◆ロッカーの利用　　Use of lockers

User（U）：ロッカーの使い方がわかりません。

> I don't know how to use the lockers.

Librarian（L）：鍵はロッカーについています。100円硬貨を入れて鍵をかけてください。硬貨は利用がすめば返却されます。

> The key is attached to the locker. Insert a 100 yen coin and lock the locker. Your coin will be refunded after you surrender the locker.

筆記用具のみ持ち込み可です。それ以外はロッカーに入れてください。

> Writing implements are permitted in the reading room. Other objects must be placed in a locker.

備え付けのビニール袋をご利用ください。

　　Please use the provided plastic bags.

ロッカー室の出入りの際は係員に手荷物をご提示ください。

　　When you enter or leave the locker room, show your belongings to the person on duty.

施設案内　Guide to the facilities

◆蔵書構成案内　**Overview of the collection**

Librarian：蔵書数は約 10 万冊です。

There are a hundred thousand volumes in the library.

雑誌は約○○タイトルを購入しています。

We subscribe to ○○ periodical titles.

外国語図書の割合は 4 割ほどです。

The proportion of foreign language books is about 40%.

英字新聞は 4 紙とっています。

We receive four English language newspapers.

児童書には英語で書かれたものもあります。

There are also some children's books in English.

すべて開架式になっています。

All the materials are in open stacks.

地階は閉架書庫になっています。教員の方は入庫できます。

The basement stacks are closed. But faculty members can enter the stacks.

閉架書庫の資料の利用は，カウンターに相談してください。

Please ask at the counter to use the materials in the closed stacks.

◆フロア案内　**Floor guide**

〈比較的小さな図書館で案内図のある場合　Smaller libraries〉

Librarian：今いらっしゃる場所はここです。

This is where you are now.

外国語図書はここに配架してあります。

Foreign language books are shelved here.

1階には新聞・雑誌・児童書があります。

Newspapers, magazines, and children's books are on the first floor.

2階には単行本とレファレンスカウンター，レファレンスブックがあります。

Monographs, reference counters, and reference books are on the second floor.

地下にホール，食堂／喫茶，貸し会議室があります。

A hall, a restaurant/coffee shop, and a rental meeting room are in the basement.

地域資料室は1階の東側にあります。

The local collections room is on the eastern side of the first floor.

トイレは入口のそばにあります。

The restrooms are near the entrance.

赤いカーペットの敷いてある1段高くなったところからが，児童室のコーナーです。

The red carpet covering the raised area is the children's section.

児童室にある「おはなしのへや」では，毎週水曜日に本

の読み聞かせが行われています。

> In the children's section, there is a story-telling room where books are read aloud every Wednesday.

閲覧室は飲食禁止です。ただし，蓋つきの飲み物は持ち込みいただけます。飲食できるところは1階のロビーに限ります。

> Eating and drinking are not permitted in the reading room, but you can bring your own beverages with lids. Eating and drinking are permitted only in the lobby on the first floor.

靴を脱いで利用してください。

> Please remove your shoes before you go in.

〈大きな図書館や，建物が2つ以上ある図書館　Large libraries or libraries with more than one building〉

Librarian（L）：今いらっしゃるのは別館です。

> You are now in the annex.

旧館へは，3階に連絡通路があります。

> A connecting walkway to the old building is on the third floor.

別館への連絡通路はあちらです。

> A connecting walkway to the annex is over there.

2号棟の入口は建物の北側です。

> The entrance to wing number two is on the northern side of the building.

OPAC 端末は各階に備えています。

> OPAC terminals are available on each floor.

学生用／教員用の閲覧室は2階と3階にあります。

The student/faculty reading rooms are on the second and third floors.

2階へ行くには，出口側の階段をお使いください。

To reach the second floor, use the stairs on the exit side.

トイレは各階の階段の脇にあります。

The restrooms are on each floor near the stairs.

新聞閲覧室は別館4階です。

The newspaper reading room is on the fourth floor of the annex.

貸出カウンターは本館2階です。

The book circulation counter is on the second floor of the main building.

雑誌カウンターは別館の2階にあります。

The periodicals circulation counter is on the second floor of the annex.

法令関係資料室は，別館の5階です。

The legislative materials room is on the fifth floor of the annex.

閲覧室／参考図書室／複写カウンターはあちらです。

The reading room/reference room/photocopying counter is over there.

展示室はここからまっすぐ行って右奥にあります。

The exhibition room is straight ahead from here and on the far-right side.

ご自身のパソコンやタブレットを使える席は1階から3階までです。電源も自由に使えます。無料のWi-Fiもあ

ります。パスワードは壁に掲示しています。

You can use your own computer or tablet on the first to third floors. You are free to use the power outlets. Free Wi-Fi is also available. The password is posted on the wall.

ラーニングコモンズは2階の南側にあります。

The Learning Commons is located on the southern side of the second floor.

館内でのタブレット端末／プロジェクター／ホワイトボードの貸出は，3階カウンターで受け付けています。学生証／教職員証を持参してください。

Please apply at the third-floor counter for a tablet/projector/whiteboard loan. Please bring your student/faculty ID.

User：どうもありがとう。この地図（フロアマップ／利用案内）をいただけますか？

Thank you. May I have this map（floor map/library usage guide）?

L：はい。差し上げます。

Yes, you can keep it.

L：申し訳ありませんが，差し上げることができません。

I'm sorry. I can't give it to you.

◆施設の利用と予約　　　**Use of facilities and making reservations**

User（U）：グループ学習室の使用を申し込みたいのですが，どのような手続きが必要ですか？

I'd like to apply to use a group study room. Can you

施設案内………11

tell me what steps I would need to take after this?

Librarian（L）: この予約表を見てください。いつご利用になりますか？

Please look at this reservation schedule. When do you want to use it?

U: 今です。

Now.

L: すみません。今は全部使用中です。午後なら大丈夫です。

Sorry. They're all currently in use. Some are available in the afternoon.

授業時間の2時限まで予約することができます。

You can reserve a room for up to two class periods.

丸1日の利用の申込みはここでは受け付けられません。総合カウンターにご相談ください。

Here we can't approve an application to use it for an entire day. Please ask at the general counter.

今日はすべて埋まっています。明日以降の予約は学内ポータルから申し込んでください。

All rooms are booked today. Please make reservations for tomorrow or later through the campus portal.

U: では午後予約します。

I'd like to reserve it for the afternoon.

L: この用紙に記入してください。

Please complete this form.

鍵をお渡ししますので，ここにいらしてください。

We'll provide you with the key later. Please collect it from here.

12 ········ I　カウンターやフロアでの簡単な案内

L：図書館利用者カードを使って，専用端末からお申し込みください。

> Please use your library card to apply using the dedicated terminal.

キャンセルの場合は同じ端末からキャンセル手続きをしてください。

> If you wish to cancel, please proceed with the cancellation procedure at the same terminal.

キャンセルする場合は，必ずご連絡をお願いします。

> Please inform us if you decide not to use it.

User：研究個室を利用したいです。

> I'd like to use a cubicle.

Librarian：予約制になっています。

> We use a reservation system.

今ですと，Ａの研究個室でしたら空いています。

> Currently, Cubicle A is available.

研究個室は1週間単位でお貸ししています。

> Cubicles are assigned for a one-week period.

Ｂの研究個室が来週火曜日から利用できます。

> Cubicle B will be available from next Tuesday.

資料別案内　　　Guidance by type of material

◆単行本，雑誌，新聞，他資料の配架場所　　Locations of monographs, periodicals, newspapers, and other materials

User（U）：これらの資料の配架場所を教えていただけますか？

>Can you tell me where these materials are?

Librarian（L）：まず，この案内書をご覧ください。

>First check this guide please.

配架場所について簡単に説明します。

>I'll briefly explain about shelving.

書名のアルファベット順に並んでいます。

>Titles are in alphabetical order.

書名の前に書かれた数字は請求記号です。

>The numbers written in front of the title are call numbers.

U：この本とこれらの雑誌を探しています。どうしたら見つかりますか？

>I'm searching for this book and these periodicals. How can I find them?

L：では，まずOPAC で調べてください。

>Well, first please check the OPAC.

単行本は日本十進分類法に従って分類され，書架に並んでいます。

>Monographs are classified and shelved according to the Nippon Decimal Classification.

辞書類，百科事典類は窓際に別置されています。

Dictionaries and encyclopedias are shelved by the windows.

User（U）：この本はどこにありますか？（請求記号がわかっている）

Where is this book?（Call number is known.）

Librarian（L）：2 階の南側にこの番号順に並んでいます。

On the second floor, south side, in numerical order.

L：この本は書庫にあるため，係員がお持ちします。

This book is in the closed stack, so staff will retrieve it for you.

OPAC で申し込んでください。

Please apply for it on the OPAC.

本が届きましたら，電光掲示板にこの番号が表示されますので取りにきてください。20 分程度でご用意できるかと思います。

When the book arrives, this number will be displayed on the electronic bulletin board. Then come to collect the book. It will take about 20 minutes to prepare the book.

L：OPAC の所在に「自動書庫」と表示されている場合，アイコンをクリックしてください。申込み後，必ず出庫依頼票を印刷してお持ちください。

If the OPAC location is displayed as "Automated Storage and Retrieval," click the icon. After applying, please print the request form for the stacks and submit

資料別案内⋯⋯⋯15

it to the library staff.

L：この本は別館の書庫にあるので，取り寄せになります。

This book is in storage in the annex. Delivery will take some time.

明日の午後 2 時過ぎなら利用ができますが，申し込みされますか？

We'll have it for you after 2:00 p.m. tomorrow. Is that all right?

L：この本は法令資料室にあります。カウンターがありますから，そこでお尋ねください。

This book is in the legislative materials room. They have their own counter. Please ask there.

L：請求記号の前にアスタリスクのついている大型本はそれぞれの書架の最後にあります。

An asterisk in front of the call number indicates that the item is an oversized book shelved at the end of each stack.

User（U）：雑誌はどこにありますか？

Where are the periodicals/magazines/journals?

Librarian（L）：これは雑誌のリストです。

Here is the periodicals list.

図書館で所蔵しているすべての雑誌と逐次刊行物の請求記号，所蔵事項，書架番号を調べることができます。

This list contains all periodicals held by our library; it lists the call number, holdings, and shelf number for each title.

雑誌のタイトルのアルファベット順にリストされています。

The titles are listed in an alphabetical order.

L：すべて開架書架にあります。

They are all in the open stacks.

3階の雑誌室で利用できます。

You can use them in the periodicals room on the third floor.

最近1年分はラウンジに，バックナンバーは閉架書庫にあります。

Issues for the last 12 months are in the lounge; back numbers are in the closed stacks.

日本の雑誌は五十音順（あいうえお順）に配架してあります。

Japanese periodicals are shelved in the order of Japanese syllabaries（a, i, u, e, o order）.

外国の雑誌はアルファベット順に配架してあります。

Foreign periodicals are arranged in alphabetical order.

国内雑誌と外国雑誌はアルファベット順に混配してあります。

Japanese and foreign periodicals are inter-shelved in alphabetical order.

製本雑誌は1階／層のW1から始まり，書庫1から4階／層まで配架されています。

The bound periodicals begin at W1 on the first floor/ level and are shelved up to the fourth floor/level.

新着雑誌は1階に配架されています。

資料別案内⋯⋯⋯17

The current issues of periodicals are shelved on the first floor.

新着雑誌はここに1週間展示後，他の部署へ回覧します。

Current issues of periodicals are displayed for one week and then circulated to various departments.

展示後は未製本棚へ配架します。

After the display period, they are moved to the unbound periodicals shelves.

未製本雑誌は閲覧室にあります。

The unbound periodicals are in the reading room.

製本雑誌は地下書庫へ配架します。

The bound periodicals are shelved in the basement stacks.

雑誌はここに書いてあるとおり，出版年によって配架してあります。

-1980	4階
1981-2000	3階
2001-2020	2階
2021- 現在	1階

As is written here, periodicals are shelved according to the year of publication.

Up to 1980	4th floor
1981-2000	3rd floor
2001-2020	2nd floor
2021-Present	1st floor

U：新聞はどうなっていますか？

What about the newspapers?

L：新聞は1週間分が閲覧室に配架されています。

Newspapers are shelved in the reading room for a week.

それ以前の古い新聞は閉架書庫にあります。

Older newspapers are in the closed stacks.

今日の朝刊はすべて入口ホールの新聞閲覧台に綴じられています。

This morning's papers are all in the newspaper racks in the entrance hall.

あそこの新聞架にかかっているのが今日の朝刊です。

Today's morning papers are on those rods.

昨日以前のものは原紙を 15 日ずつ紐綴じにして新聞架に入れてあります。

The ones before yesterday's are fastened in groups of fifteen days and kept on newspaper shelves.

2010 年の『人民日報』は縮刷版で所蔵しています。

The 2010 issues of the *People's Daily* are held in the reduced-size edition.

1993 年の『ニューヨーク・タイムズ』はマイクロフィルムで所蔵しています。

The 1993 issues of the *New York Times* are held in microfilms.

マイクロフィッシュとマイクロフィルムは閲覧室のキャビネットに保管されています。

Microfiches and microfilms are kept in cabinets in the reading room.

デジタル資料は，指定の端末で閲覧できます。

You can access digital materials on designated devices in the library.

資料別案内········19

User：この付近の地図がありますか？

    Do you have maps showing this area?

Librarian（L）：レファレンスカウンターに備えてあります。

    They are at the reference counter.

L：地域資料室の書架の上においてあります。

    They are on the top of the shelves in the local collections room.

L：地図室には住宅地図があります。

    The map room has maps of the residential area.

  ロードマップでしたら，目録を調べれば貸出できるものがあるはずです。

    If you are looking for road maps, a search of the catalog will probably generate road maps to borrow.

各種サービス　　Guidance by type of service

◆複写　　**Photocopying**

User：図書館の本を複写できますか？

Can I photocopy library books?

Librarian：まず，この案内書をお読みください。

First read this explanation.

複写には著作権法による制限があります。

Copyright laws limit photocopying.

全体のページ数の半分以下しか複写できません。

Less than half of the total pages of an item can be copied.

複写の種類と料金はこの表のとおりです。

The types of copying and their costs are listed below.

Librarian（L）：係員がコピーします。複写カウンターに申し込んでください。

Our staff will make the photocopy for you. Apply at the photocopying counter.

User（U）：それでいつ受け取ることができますか？

When can I receive the copy?

L：待ち時間は 10 分から 30 分くらいです。

The waiting time is from ten to thirty minutes.

L：午前中に申し込んだ場合は午後渡しですが，午後受付のものは翌日渡しになります。

If you make a request in the morning, you can receive

各種サービス………21

the copy in the afternoon. Items requested in the
afternoon will be ready the following day.

こちらが受付番号になります。カウンターに掲示のある
番号までのものができあがっています。

This is your number. The numbers flashed at the counter
indicate the copies completed.

U：料金は？

How much?

L：白黒は 1 枚 30 円，カラーは 1 枚 50 円です。

It costs 30 yen for a monochrome copy and 50 yen for
a color copy per sheet.

U：キャッシュレス決済はできますか？

Can I make a cashless payment?

L：一部のクレジットカード，交通系 IC カード，バーコード
決済に対応しています。

We accept certain credit cards, transportation IC cards,
and barcode payments at our library.

L：できません。現金のみです。

I'm sorry, but we only accept cash.

Librarian：この本は傷みが激しいため，複写禁止になってい
ます。

As this book is seriously damaged, it cannot be copied.

これをもとにあった棚に戻してください。

Please return this to the shelf it came from.

User：コピーをとりたいです。

I'd like to make some copies.

Librarian：セルフサービスのコピー機を利用してください。

Please use the self-service copy machine.

コピーカード式ですので，コピー機脇に備え付けの自動販売機で購入してください。現金でのコピーは複写カウンターでお受けしています。

You need a copy card, so you'll have to buy a card from the vending machine beside the copy machine. If you want to pay cash for the copies, visit the photocopying counter.

User：セルフコピー機はどこにありますか？

Where is the self-service copy machine?

Librarian（L）：2階の書架の右側で3台利用できます。

On the second floor to the right of the shelves there are three machines.

L：コイン式のセルフサービスのコピー機があります。コピー機の脇に両替機があります。小銭をご用意ください。

There is a coin-operated self-service copy machine. There is a money changer beside the copy machines. You'll need small change.

Pref. Lee（U）：私は Lee 教授ですが，*Nature* はいつから所蔵しているか教えてください。

I'm Professor Lee. When do your holdings of *Nature* begin?

各種サービス………23

Librarian（L）：所蔵の状況を調べますので，少々お待ちくだ
さい。

I'll check the holdings. One moment, please.

1976 年以降です。

Since 1976.

U：複写はできますか？

Can I get a photocopy?

L：はい，できます。

Yes, you can.

U：それはよかった。1979 年の 282 号の論文のコピーがほし
いです。

That's good. I'd like a copy of an article in issue number
282 published in 1979.

L：タイトルとページを教えてください。

Please tell me the article title and the page numbers.

U：はい。S. W. Richardson と E. R. Oxburgh の "The heat flow
field in mainland UK" です。ページはわかりません。

Yes. It's "The heat flow field in mainland UK" by S. W.
Richardson and E. R. Oxburgh. I don't know about the
pages.

L：わかりました。現物を確認しますので少々お待ちください。

That's all right. Please wait a moment while I confirm
that we have the item.

お待たせしました。ありました。

Thank you for waiting. We do have it.

U：費用を教えてください。

How much will it cost?

24········ I　カウンターやフロアでの簡単な案内

L：教職員と学生は 1 枚につき 30 円です。

> For both faculty and students, it's 30 yen per page.

U：支払方法は？

> How do I pay?

L：複写物を取りにいらしたときに，カウンターでお支払いください。

> Please pay at the counter when you come to collect the article.

◆マイクロフィルムの複写　　Copies from microfilms

User（U）：マイクロフィルムのコピーはできますか？

> Can you make paper copies from microfilms?

Librarian（L）：ええ，もちろん。マイクロフィルムリーダーの中にコピーができるものがあります。

> Yes, certainly. Paper copies can be obtained from some of the microfilm readers.

U：どのリーダーですか？

> Which ones?

L：この機械はコピーできます。

> This machine can make copies.

U：マイクロフィルムリーダーの使い方がわかりません。

> I don't know how to use the microfilm reader.

L：では，操作方法をお教えします。

> Now, let me show you how to operate it.

備え付けのマニュアルをご覧ください。わからなければ職員をお呼びください。

> Please refer to the manual provided. If you are unsure

各種サービス………25

how to operate it, please ask a library staff.

◆コピー機のトラブル　　　　**Problems with the photocopying machine**

User：閲覧室のコピー機が故障しています。

　　　　The copy machine in the reading room isn't working.

Librarian（L）：どうしましたか？

　　　　What's wrong?

　　　紙詰まりですね。少々お待ちください。

　　　　The paper is stuck. Please wait a moment.

　　　はい，直りました。

　　　　OK, it's fixed.

　　　返金が必要でしたらお支払いします。

　　　　You can have your money refunded if you wish.

L：そうですか。ちょっと見てみましょう。

　　　　Is that right? Let me see.

　　これは修理を依頼する必要があります。

　　　　The copy machine needs to be repaired.

　　事務室のコピー機をお使いください。

　　　　Please use the one in the office.

◆購入希望　　**Request for the purchase of a book**

User：図書館にない本を購入してほしいのですが，リクエストはできますか？

　　　　I'd like the library to buy books that it doesn't have. Can I make a request?

26………Ⅰ　カウンターやフロアでの簡単な案内

Librarian（L）：この図書館の利用資格のある方は誰でも購入依頼を出すことができます。

Anyone qualified to use this library can request for the purchase of a book.

購入依頼を出した方は，その資料の到着後優先的に利用することができます。

The person who requests the book receives priority in using it when it arrives.

資料が到着次第，連絡を差し上げます。

We notify you when the material arrives.

資料は到着後展示されますが，その後は申し込んだ方が優先的に貸出を受けることができます。

The book is displayed on arrival, but, after that, the person who requested it receives priority in checking it out.

外国雑誌は取引書店との契約の関係上，年始めか次に刊行される巻の初号からの購入になります。

According to the contract with the foreign periodicals dealer, subscriptions begin with the first issue of the year or the first issue of the next volume.

利用できるまでだいたい 2 週間から 3 週間かかります。

It will be available for use in a few weeks.

研究費からの購入をご希望でしたら，図書館ではなく庶務課にお申し込みください。

If you would like to pay with your research allowance, the order is handled by the General Affairs section rather than the library.

各種サービス………27

L：購入依頼のあった資料が利用できるようになりました。

> The materials you asked to be ordered are available for use.

貸出カウンターまでお越しください。8月31日まで取り置きます。

> Please come to the circulation counter. It will be held until August 31.

L：購入依頼のあった資料は，残念ながら絶版で購入できませんでした。

> The material you requested for is out of print and could not be purchased.

L：購入依頼のあった資料について，確認したい点がございます。お手数ですが，図書館の杉本まで連絡ください。

> We would like to confirm some information regarding the requested items. Please contact Sugimoto at the library.

L：購入依頼のあった資料はすでに所蔵しております。請求記号は○○○です。

> The material you suggested for library purchase is already in the collection. Its call number is ○○○.

L：購入依頼のあった資料は，残念ながら当図書館の収書方針と照らし合わせた結果購入できません。レファレンス担当者にご相談くだされば，他館の所蔵をお調べします。

> The material you requested for is beyond the scope of our collection policy. If you consult our reference staff, it may be possible to check the holdings at another library.

28········ I　カウンターやフロアでの簡単な案内

◆障害者サービス　Service for the persons with disabilities

(1)　図書館に来館することが困難な方に，図書の宅配サービスをしています。

> Home delivery services are available for people who are unable to visit libraries.

(2)　図書館には，点字図書，布の絵本，DAISY，大活字本などがあります。

> The library has braille books, cloth picture books, DAISY, and large-print books.

(3)　障害をお持ちの方のために，所蔵資料の電子化（テキスト化）を依頼することができます。

> Users with disabilities can request the digitization (text conversion) of the materials in our collection.

◆団体貸出　Group loans

(1)　地域の保育園・学童クラブ・高齢者施設などにまとめて図書を貸出するサービスです。

> We offer group loan to local nursery schools, school children's clubs, and facilities for the elderly.

(2)　一度に□冊○か月借りられます。配送のサービスもあります。

> In a single transaction, □ books can be borrowed for ○ months. Delivery service is also available.

退館　　Leaving the library

◆入退館ゲートが鳴ったら　　**Stopped by book detection system**

Librarian（L）：ID カードをゲートにタッチしてお通りください。

Please pass through the gate by holding your ID over the card reader.

User：ゲートが開きません。

The gate won't open.

L：貸出手続の済んでいない本はありませんか？

Do you have any books that haven't been checked out?

何か金属製のものをお持ちですか？

Do you have anything made of metal?

折りたたみの傘やスマートフォン，タブレットなどをお持ちですか？

Do you have a folding umbrella, smartphone, or tablet?

この傘をカウンターに預かりますので，もう一度ゲートを通ってください。

Let me hold this umbrella at the counter. Please pass through the gate again.

L：恐れ入りますが，バッグの中を見せてください。

May I see what is in the bag?

館外貸出はできませんので，借りたところに返してきてください。

This cannot be taken out of the library. Please return it

30········ I　カウンターやフロアでの簡単な案内

> to where you borrowed it from.

ご協力ありがとうございました。

> Thank you for your cooperation.

L：資料を無断で持ち出した場合，図書館利用を一定期間停止することがあります。

> If you try to remove something improperly from the library, library privileges may be suspended for a certain period.

非常時　　　In case of emergency

◆地震が発生したら　　**In case of earthquake**

Librarian：地震が発生しました。書架から離れてください。

An earthquake has occurred. Please move away from the bookshelves.

安全なところへ逃げてください。エレベーターは使えません。

Seek safety in secure areas. Elevators are not operational.

前の人を押さないでください。職員の誘導に従って，順番に階段を下りてください。

Please do not push a person in front of you. Follow the staff's guidance and descend the stairs in an orderly manner.

◆火災が発生したら　　**In case of fire**

Librarian（L）：火事です。6階の食堂で火災が発生しました。

The library is on fire. A fire has occurred in the cafeteria on the sixth floor.

職員の指示に従って，避難してください。エレベーターは使えません。

Please evacuate according to staff instructions. Elevators are not operational.

L：ただ今，1階で火災報知器が鳴っています。現在，状況を確認しておりますので，職員の指示があるまでお待ちください。

> We have received a fire alarm notification on the first floor. We are currently checking the situation, so please await further instructions from the staff.

電話による問い合わせ

Inquiries by telephone

電話を取ったらあわてずに
Responding without losing your composure

(1) はい，こちらは○○図書館です。

Hello, this is ○○ Library.

(2) どちらさまでしょうか。

Please tell me your name.

(3) お声が聞き取りづらいので，もう少し大きな声で話してください。

I'm afraid I can't hear you very well, please speak a little louder.

(4) もう少しゆっくり話してください。

Please speak slowly.

(5) すみませんが，私は英語がわかりませんので，他の者に代わります。

I'm sorry I cannot speak English well. Let me connect you with someone else.

(6) 少々お待ちください。

Please hold the line for a moment.

(7) 図書館の利用についてくわしくは，当館のウェブサイトをご覧ください。

For more information on using the library, please refer to our library website.

利用資格の確認　　　　Determining qualifications of user

◆利用資格に制限がない場合（公共図書館等） **When the library has no rules qualifying users（such as public libraries）**

User：図書館を利用したいのですが，誰でも利用できますか？

I'd like to use the library. Can anyone use it?

Librarian：はい，どなたでも利用できます。

Yes, anyone may use this library.

ただし，貸出は，○○市（区・町・村）に在住，在学，在勤の方または隣接市に在住の方に限ります。

However, borrowing materials is available only to those who live, study, or work in ○○ city（ward, town, village）or adjacent cities.

◆利用資格に制限がある場合（大学・専門図書館等） **In the case of any eligibility restrictions for library use（such as universities or special libraries）**

User（U）：もしもし，○○図書館ですか？

Hello, is this ○○ Library?

Librarian（L）：はい，こちらは○○図書館です。ご用件は？

Yes, this is ○○ Library. How may I help you?

U：私は○○大学（会社）の学生／研究員です。

I am a student/researcher at ○○ University.

I work for ○○ Company.

図書館を利用できますか？

Can I use the library?

L：申し訳ございませんが，外部の方の利用はできません。

I'm sorry but people from outside cannot use this library.

所属の図書館から紹介状をもらってきてください。

Please bring a letter of introduction from the library at your institution.

U：そちらの大学の医学部の斎藤先生から推薦状／紹介状をいただいています。

I have a letter of recommendation/introduction from Prof. Saito of the Faculty of Medicine of your university.

L：わかりました。

I understand.

ではご来館ください。

You will be able to use the library.

交通機関・経路　　　Transportation

User（U）：そちらの図書館へはどのように行けばよいでしょうか？

How can I reach your library?

U：駅からどのくらいかかりますか？

How far is it from the station?

Librarian（L）：最寄りの駅は○○です。

The nearest station is ○○ station.

西口に出てください。

Use the west exit.

X 番の出口から出てください。

Use exit number X.

○○駅前から X 番の●●行きのバスに乗車して，◇◇で下車してください。

In front of ○○ station, catch the number X bus bound for ●●. Get off at ◇◇.

駅／バス停から歩いて 10 分です。

It is a 10 minutes' walk from the station/bus stop.

大学の構内に入ったら，受付に図書館の場所を尋ねてください。

When you reach the university campus, ask at the reception desk where the library is located.

Library は日本語で「図書館」といいます。

The Japanese word for library is *toshokan.*

L：電話で説明するのは難しいのですが，駅には英文併記の付近の地図があります。それに載っているはずです。

> It can be difficult to provide direction over the telephone. But, there is a map near the station with place-names in English; that should be helpful.

L：大学のウェブサイトにキャンパスマップがあります。図書館は○番の●階です。

> You can find a campus map on the university website. The library is located on the ● floor of building number ○.

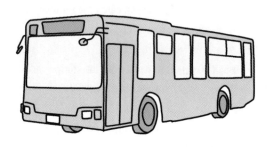

開館のお知らせ　　Service hours

◆開館時間　　**Opening hours**

User（U）：開館日と開館時間を教えていただけませんか？

Please tell me the working days and hours for the library.

U：図書館の開館時間を教えていただけませんか？

Please tell me when the library is open.

U：では，土曜日と日曜日は？

What about Saturday and Sunday?

U：今晩何時に閉館ですか？

What time does the library close tonight?

Librarian（L）：月曜日から金曜日までは午前 9 時から午後 9 時までです。

From Monday to Friday, the library is open from 9:00 a.m. to 9:00 p.m.

L：開館時間は，月曜日から金曜日までは午前 10 時から午後 5 時までです。

The library is open Monday through Friday from 10:00 a.m. to 5:00 p.m.

土曜日は午前 9 時から午後 4 時までです。

For Saturday, the working hours are 9:00 a.m. to 4:00 p.m.

日曜と祝日は休館です。

The library is closed on Sundays and holidays.

L：日曜日以外は午後 9 時まで開館しています。

Except Sunday, the library is open every night until 9:00 p.m.

L：24 時間利用できます。

It is open 24 hours a day.

年中無休です。

It is open year-round.

L：毎月第 1 木曜日と第 3 日曜日は休館です。

On the first Thursday and third Sunday of the month, the library is closed.

L：開館時間は曜日によって異なります。

The open hours differ according to the day of the week.

月曜日は午後 1 時から午後 8 時まで，火曜日から金曜日までは午前 9 時 30 分から午後 8 時までです。

On Monday, the hours are from 1:00 p.m. to 8:00 p.m., and from Tuesday through Friday, the hours are from 9:30 a.m. to 8:00 p.m.

土曜，日曜，祝祭日は午前 9 時 30 分から午後 5 時までです。

On Saturdays, Sundays, and holidays, the hours are 9:30 a.m. to 5:00 p.m.

◆休館・閉館　**Closure**

Librarian（L）：土曜日と祝日の翌日は休館です。

On Saturday and the day after a holiday, the library is closed.

月末は蔵書点検のため休館します。

At the end of the month, the library is closed for

42·········Ⅱ　電話による問い合わせ

inventory.

7月末から8月末までの夏期休暇期間は日曜休館です。

During summer vacation from late July until the end of August, the library is closed on Sundays.

複写サービスは午後5時までです。

Photocopying service is provided until 5:00 p.m.

書庫資料の請求受付時間は午後4時までです。

The deadline for requesting materials from the closed stack is 4:00 p.m.

初めて利用される方は午後4時30分までにいらしてください。

First-time users should arrive by 4:30 p.m.

L：台風の接近に伴い，明日午後1時まで臨時休館します。正午時点で特別警報が発令されている場合，終日休館とします。最新の情報は当館ウェブサイトでご確認ください。

Owing to the approaching typhoon, the library will be temporarily closed until 1:00 p.m. tomorrow. If an emergency warning is issued by noon, the library will remain closed for the entire day. Please refer to our website for the latest updates.

L：システム更新のため，2025年12月15日から2026年1月5日まで臨時休館します。期間中は，図書館ウェブサイトを含む図書館の全システムは利用できないため，Web，お電話等での検索・予約・延長等はお受けできません。

Owing to system updates, the library will be temporarily closed from December 15th, 2025 to January 5th, 2026. During this period, all library systems, including the library websites, will be unavailable. Therefore, we will not be able to assist with searches, reservations, extensions, or any other services via the web or by telephone.

L：1階の耐震補強工事に伴い，児童室を閉室します。この期間，2階以上のフロアは通常通り開館し，臨時ミニ児童室を3階研修室に開設します。

Owing to the seismic reinforcement work on the first floor, the children's section will be closed. During this period, the second floors and above the first floor will remain open as usual, and a temporary small children's section will be set up in the third floor training room.

訪問の約束　　　　An appointment to visit the library

Dr. Paton（U）：もしもし，私はカナダから来た Dr. Paton です。来週神戸で開催される〇〇学会に出席するために日本にきております。東京にいる間,貴図書館やいくつかの医学・薬学図書館を見学したいと思っています。

> Hello, my name is Dr. Paton. I'm from Canada. I've come to Japan to participate in the 〇〇 Society meeting in Kobe the following week. I'd like to visit your library as well as other medical and pharmaceutical libraries while I'm in Tokyo.

Mr. Takano（L）：そうですか。図書館見学の目的を教えていただけませんか？

> I see. In particular, what would you like to examine at our library?

U：そうですね。図書館をひとまわりして利用の方法を知りたいです。訪問の約束はできますか？

> Well, I'd like to take a general look from the user's viewpoint. Can I make an appointment?

L：はい，明朝 10 時はいかがでしょう？

> Yes, you can. How about 10 o'clock tomorrow morning?

U：スケジュールの都合で，今日の午後 2 時ごろうかがってもよろしいでしょうか。

> Considering my schedule, I'd like to do it at about 2:00 p.m. today.

訪問の約束………45

L：大丈夫です。

That would be all right.

U：では，今日 2 時ごろうかがいます。

Then I'll be there today at around 2 o'clock.

L：申し訳ございませんが，本日は都合がつきません。

We apologize, but we are not available today owing to prior commitments.

L：担当者が不在のため，ご希望の時間には対応できません。都合のよい時間をいくつか教えていただけますか？

We apologize, but the person in charge is currently unavailable. So, we will not be able to assist you at your preferred time. Can you please provide us with alternative time options that would be convenient?

L：図書館の場所はわかりますか？

Do you know where the library is?

U：はい。

Yes, I do.

L：それはよかった。

That's good.

U：あなたのお名前を教えていただけますか？

Could you tell me your name?

L：司書の高野といいます。

I'm a librarian and my name is Takano.

U：ありがとう。じゃあその時に。

Thank you. See you then.

移動図書館の巡回スポット　　　Bookmobile

User（U）：図書館に行くことができないのですが，図書館を
利用する方法があれば教えていただけますか？

I can't visit the library in person. Is there another way
to use the library?

Librarian（L）：移動図書館をご存じですか？

Do you know about the bookmobile?

市内／区内／町内を車で巡回移動する移動図書館です。

It is a mobile library that stops throughout the city/
ward/town.

蔵書は○○冊程度です。

It carries about ○○ volumes.

月に／週に○○回の割合で巡回しています。

Each month/week, it makes ○○ trips along the route.

市内／区内／町内に拠点が何か所かあります。

Within the city/ward/town, it makes several stops.

住所を教えてください。

Please provide your address.

U：○○です。

I live in ○○.

L：お住まいに一番近い拠点は○○です。

The closest stop to your address is ○○.

ここへは火曜日の午後 3 時に移動図書館が巡回してきます。

The bookmobile will come by 3:00 p.m. on Tuesday.

図書館利用者カードをすでにお持ちなら，それを利用できます。

If you already have a library card, you can use it.

L：図書館利用者カードは別に必要になります。

A separate library card is required.

利用方法は移動図書館が来たときに，直接聞いてください。

The bookmobile staff can explain how to use it.

忘れ物　　Lost and found

User（U）：先日うかがったときに傘を忘れたようなのですが，届いていませんか？

When I was at your library the other day, I forgot my umbrella. Is it still there?

Librarian（L）：どのような傘ですか？

Could you describe it?

U：黒で，木の柄のもので，イニシャルがTKLと入っています。

Black, with a wooden handle, and the initials TKL.

L：少々お待ちください。今調べます。

Please hold the line a moment. I'll check.

はい，ありました。

Yes, it's here.

お名前をうかがえますか？

May I have your name?

すみませんが，スペルを教えてください。

Please spell it.

受付カウンターに取り置きますので，取りにいらしてください。

It will be at the reception counter. You can collect it from there.

L：残念ながら届いていません。

I'm sorry, it's not here.

貸出・返却

Circulation

登録　　Registration

◆**公共図書館**　**Public libraries**

User（U）：初めて貸出を受けるのですが，手続きの方法を教えてください。

This is the first time for me to borrow books here. Please explain the process.

Librarian（L）：今，住所を証明するものをお持ちですか？

Do you have any identification that shows your address?

U：どんなものを見せればよいですか？

What sort of identification would you like to see?

L：在留カードまたは特別永住者証明書はお持ちですか？

Do you have a residence card or special permanent resident certificate that you can present at the library?

U：はい，持っています。

Yes, I do.

L：拝見してよろしいですか？

May I see it?

U：どうぞ。

Here it is.

L：お住まいは市外／区／町／県ですね。

So you live outside the city/ward/town/prefecture.

お住まいが市内／区／町／県の方でないと，登録できません。

Unless you live within the city/ward/town/prefecture, you cannot register.

勤務先か通学先は市内／区／町／県ですか？

Do you work or attend school within the city/ward/town/prefecture?

社員証などはお持ちですか？

Do you have company identification with you now?

U：持っています。

Yes, I do.

L：では，新規に発行しますので，この登録用紙に記入してください。

Then we'll issue you a new one. Please complete this registration form.

ここにお名前，住所，電話番号をご記入ください。

Please provide your name, address and telephone number.

こちらに会社名，所在地，電話番号を記入してください。

Please provide your company's name, address and telephone number.

はい，それでけっこうです。

OK, that's fine.

お待たせしました。こちらが図書館利用者カードです。在留カード／特別永住者証明書をお返しします。

Thank you for waiting. Here is your library card. I'll return your residence card/special permanent resident certificate.

登録········53

◆大学図書館　**University libraries**

User（U）：貸出のための利用登録をしたいです。

I want to register to borrow books.

Librarian（L）：学生証／職員証をお持ちですか？

学生証／職員証は図書館利用者カードとして利用できます。

Do you have your student/staff ID?

You can use the student/staff ID as a library card.

U：私はこの大学に来たばかりで，学生証／職員証を持っていません。

I've recently joined this university and don't have a student/staff ID yet.

L：この紙に学籍番号と名前を記入してください。

Please provide your student number and name.

U：私は科目等履修生ですが，利用登録できますか？

I am a non-degree student. Can I register with the library?

L：科目等履修生の方にはこちらで図書館利用者カードを発行します。科目等履修生証を貸していただけますか？

We issue library cards to non-degree students. Can I borrow your non-degree student ID card?

毎年年度始めには更新しなければなりません。

The card must be renewed at the beginning of each school year.

図書館利用者カードの更新は無料です。

There is no charge for renewal of library cards.

L：卒業生／地域住民の方には，図書館利用者カードを発行

54 ········· Ⅲ　貸出・返却

します。

> We issue library cards to graduates/local residents.

卒業証明書と身分証明書が必要です。卒業証明書は教務部で発行していますので，教務部でご確認いただけますか？

> To issue library cards, you need your graduation certificate and identification. The graduation certificate can be obtained from the Academic Affairs Office, hence, could you please ask them?

◆図書館利用者カードに関する取扱いについて　　**Rules of the library card**

(1)　このカードの有効期限は1年です。

> This card is valid for one year.

(2)　図書館利用者カードは市内／区内／町内のどの図書館でも利用できます。

> This library card is valid at any library within the city/ward/town.

(3)　本を借りるときは，このカードをお出しください。

> When you borrow a book, present this card.

(4)　図書館利用者カードを紛失しないように気をつけてください。

> Be careful not to lose your library card.

(5)　図書館利用者カードを紛失した場合は速やかにご連絡ください。

> If you do lose your library card, please notify us immediately.

(6) 卒業時／退職時／不要になったときは，必ずご返却ください。

　　When you graduate/leave a company/leave a university/no longer need it, be sure to return the card.

(7) 再発行には手数料 1,000 円かかります。

　　There is a 1,000 yen fee for reissuing cards.

(8) このカードを他人に貸すことはできません。

　　Don't allow another person to use your card.

貸出規則　　　Circulation policy

◆禁帯出資料　　Non-circulation materials

User（U）：この本は借りられますか？

　　　　　　Can I check this book out?

Librarian（L）：もちろん。開架式書架にある蔵書は 2 週間利用者に貸し出しています。

　　　　　　Certainly. Books in the open stacks may be borrowed for two weeks.

　　　　参考図書と貴重本は図書館内でしか使用できません。

　　　　　　But reference and rare books must only be used within the library.

U：雑誌の最新号は借りられますか？

　　　　　　Can the latest issue of a periodical be checked out?

L：雑誌の貸出はしておりません。

　　　　　　No, periodicals cannot be checked out.

　　この雑誌は館外貸出禁止です。

　　　　　　This periodical cannot be taken out of the library.

L：受入れ後 2 週間は貸出できません。

　　　　　　It cannot be checked out until two weeks after we receive it.

U：この辞書は貸出可能ですか？

　　　　　　Can I check out this dictionary?

L：残念ですが，赤ラベルの貼ってある参考図書は禁帯出です。閲覧室でご利用ください。

I'm sorry, but a reference book with a red label cannot be checked out. You must use it in the reading room.

◆貸出期間・貸出冊数 **Loan period and the number of items that may be borrowed**

User（U）：一度に何冊借りられますか？

How many books can I take out at one time?

Librarian（L）：貸出は雑誌も含めて1回5冊までです。

Including periodicals, you can borrow five books at one time.

U：貸出期間はどれくらいですか？

How long can I keep them out?

L：単行本は1か月，雑誌は1週間です。

Monographs may be borrowed for one month, periodicals for one week.

L：貸出冊数に制限はありません。

There is no limit to the number of items you can borrow.

L：日本語図書は5冊，外国語図書は3冊まで借りられます。

You can borrow up to five Japanese books, three foreign language books.

雑誌は館外貸出はしていません。

We don't loan periodicals for use outside the library.

L：単行本は5冊，音楽CDやDVDは2点までで2週間です。

Five monographs and two music CDs or DVDs can be borrowed for two weeks.

L：来週から大学が春休みに入るので，貸出期間は 1 か月になります。

> The loan period will be one month since the university will be on spring break, beginning next week.

L：貸出冊数と貸出期間は身分により異なります。学部生は 10 冊 2 週間，大学院生は 30 冊 3 週間です。

> The number of books and loan periods depend on status. Undergraduate students may borrow ten books for two weeks, and graduate students may borrow thirty books for three weeks.

◆罰則，延滞料　Penalties and overdue fines

User：この本を返却したいのですが，期限が過ぎてしまいました。

> I'd like to return this book. It's overdue.

Librarian（L）：貸出期間が過ぎてもそのまま持っていると，1 冊または 1 号につき 1 日 10 円の延滞料を払わなければなりません。

> If you keep something beyond the due date, you'll have to pay 10 yen per day for each book or periodical issue.

L：貸出期間が過ぎてもそのまま持っていると，新たな本が借りられません。

> If you keep a book beyond the due date, you will not be able to borrow any other books.

貸出規則………59

User：借りた本にコーヒーをこぼしてしまいました。

I spilled coffee on this book I borrowed.

Librarian（L）：では拝見します。

Let me take a look.

これはちょっと状態がよくないですね。同じ資料で弁償していただくことになっています。

This is pretty bad. You'll have to pay for the re-placement copy.

L：修理が必要だと思われます。修理費をご負担いただくことになります。

This will have to be amended. You must pay the cost of repairing it.

L：これくらいなら仕方ないですね。これからはこのようなことがないようお願いします。

That sort of thing is unavoidable. Please be careful in the future.

資料請求，館内利用　　　　Paging and reading room use

User（U）：この請求記号の本はどこにありますか？

Where can I find a book with this call number?

Librarian（L）：請求記号に H のついている本は閉架書庫になります。係員がお持ちしますので，蔵書検索からお申し込みください。／この用紙に記入して貸出カウンターにお出しください。

Call numbers with an H are for books in the closed stacks. One of the staff members will provide the book to you. Please apply through the OPAC. /Please complete this form and take it to the circulation counter.

L：この本は書庫にありますので，今持ってきます。

This book is in storage. I'll get it for you.

このメモをお借りしてよろしいでしょうか？

May I take this memo?

お待たせしました。この本は館内閲覧のみになります。

Thank you for waiting. This book can only be used in a library.

図書館利用者カードをお願いします。

May I have your library card?

館内貸出の手続きをします。

I'll check it out to you for use within the library.

L：すみません。この資料は今，別の方が館内閲覧をしています。返却されましたら，館内放送でお呼びします。

  I'm sorry, but someone else is now using this book in the library. When it is returned, we'll call your name on the paging system.

U：ではこの本はけっこうです。別の本を探します。

  Well, never mind about this book. I'll find another book.

貸出　　Checkout

◆カウンターでの手続き　**Procedures at the counter**

User（U）：この本を借りたいです。

I'd like to check out this book.

Librarian（L）：では図書館利用者カードをお出しください。

Let me have your library card.

返却期限は 7 月 29 日までになります。

It will be due on July 29.

L：今，貸出停止になっています。以前，延滞本がありません
でしたか？

Your borrowing privileges have been suspended. Did
you have an overdue earlier?

本をすでに 5 冊借りていませんか？

Do you have five books checked out already?

貸出は 5 冊までです。どれか返却しなければ，これ以上
借りられません。

The limit is five books. If you don't return one, you
won't be able to borrow another one.

L：今すでに〇冊借りているので，あと 1 冊しか借りられませ
ん。

You have already checked out 〇 books. You can check
out only one additional item.

U：では，これだけ借りることにします。

OK, I'll borrow just this.

貸出………63

U：では，この本を返して，こちらを借ります。

OK, I'll return this one and borrow this one.

User：*Nature* のこの号を研究室に持っていってもいいですか？

Can I take this issue of *Nature* to a research room?

Librarian：いいえ，逐次刊行物は貸出も持ち出しもできません。

No. Periodicals cannot be checked out or removed from this area.

コイン式コピー機が各階にありますので，使ってください。

There is a coin-operated photocopying machine on each floor. Please use one of them.

◆自動貸出機　　**Self-checkout machines**

User：この本を借りたいです。

I'd like to check out this book.

Librarian：自分で自動貸出機を使って貸出処理ができます。

You can check out books for yourself by using a self-checkout machine.

貸出機の画面をタッチしてください。

Please touch the self-checkout machine screen.

図書館利用者カードのバーコードを読み込ませてください。

Scan the barcodes on the library card.

借りたい本を台の上に置いてください。

Place the books you want to check out on the table of
the self-checkout machine.

冊数を確認してください。間違っていたら冊数を修正し
てください。

Please check the number of books. If wrong numbers
displayed, please correct the number of books.

正しく表示されていることを確認して，「借りる」ボタン
をタッチします。

Check that the number of books is displayed correctly
and touch the "Borrow" button.

本の名前と貸出期限が印刷されたレシートが印刷されま
すので，本と一緒にお持ち帰りください。

A receipt will be printed with the title of books and due
date, please bring your receipt with your books.

返却　　　　Return

User：借りた本の返却期限を教えてもらえませんか。

　　　　I don't know the due date for a book I borrowed.

Librarian：書名は何というものですか？

　　　　What is the title?

図書館利用者カードにある番号を教えてください。

　　　　Please tell me the number on your library card.

苗字を教えてください。

　　　　Please tell me your last name.

少々お待ちください。

　　　　Please wait a moment.

返却期限は 11 月 20 日までです。

　　　　It is due on November 20.

User：この本を返却します。

　　　　I'd like to return this book.

Librarian：図書館利用者カードは返却のときはいりません。

　　　　Your library card is not necessary when returning books.

確認するまでお待ちください。

　　　　Please wait for a moment while I process this.

延滞していますね。これから注意してください。

　　　　It's overdue. Please be careful in the future.

延滞した日数だけ貸出が停止されます。

> Your borrowing privileges will be suspended as many days as the book is overdue.

User：この本を返却したいのですが，期限を過ぎてしまいました。

> I'd like to return this book. It's overdue.

Librarian（L）：延滞料を払っていただかないといけません。

> You'll have to pay the overdue fine.

L：図書館が閉まっているときは，ブックポストに返却してください。

> When the library is closed, return books to the book drop.

○○駅東口にあるブックポストを利用できます。ただし，ポストに返却された図書は，返却処理までに時間がかかります。1日1回，回収をします。ただし月曜日／月曜日が祝日の場合は翌日は回収しません。

> You can use the book drop located at the eastern exit of ○○ Station. But, please note that it may take some time for the returned books to be processed. We collect books from the book drop once daily. But, we don't collect them on Mondays/on the following day, if Monday is a public holiday.

図書館が開いている時間帯は，カウンターに返却してください。

> When the library is open, please return the books to the counter.

返却………67

市外の図書館から取り寄せた本は，図書館のカウンターに返却してください。

Please return the books requested from libraries outside the city to the library counter.

予約　　Reservations

◆書架にない場合　**When the books cannot be found on the shelf**

User（U）：○○という本を借りたいのですが，書架にありません。

I'd like to borrow a book called ○○, but it's not on the shelf.

U：○○という記事を見たいのですが，書架にありません。

I'd like to see an article in ○○, but the issue I want is not on the shelf.

Librarian（L）：その本は現在貸出中です。

That book has been checked out.

U：返却されたら取り置きしてもらいたいので，予約できますか。

I'd like you to hold it for me when it comes back.

L：では，予約申込書に必要事項を記入してください。

Please complete a reservation form with the necessary information.

本が戻り次第，ご連絡差し上げます。

We will notify you when the book becomes available.

L：誰かが使用中か，返却カートの上です。

Someone may be using it or it may be on a book return cart.

間違って配架されているかもしれません。

It may be mis-shelved.

L：OPAC 端末から自分で予約できます。

Using an OPAC terminal, you can make the reservation yourself.

予約されていた本が返却されましたら，学内ポータルで通知しますので，注意してご覧ください。

When the book you requested has been returned, we will notify you through the campus portal. Please pay attention and check it.

L：自宅でも図書館のウェブサイトからログインして予約することができます。

You can reserve books from home by logging in to the library's website.

U：OPAC で整理中とある本を利用したいです。

I'd like to use a book that the OPAC says is being processed.

L：予約申込書を提出していただければ，整理してご連絡します。

Please complete a reservation form, so that we can process the book and notify you.

L：担当者に確認しますので，しばらくお待ちください。

I will check with the person in charge, so please wait for a moment.

L：残念ながら装備作業中のため本日は利用できません。1 月 15 日には利用できます。

We're sorry, but the book is currently being prepared for use. You will be able to use the books on January 15.

70········Ⅲ　貸出・返却

L：後日，電話かメールでお問い合わせください。／ご連絡します。／連絡先を教えてください。

Please contact us by phone or email at a later date.

We will contact you later by phone or email.

Could you provide your contact information?

◆電話で連絡　Notification by telephone

(1) ○○さんのお宅ですか？　○○図書館と申しますが，○○さんはいらっしゃいますか？

Is this the ○○ residence? I'm calling from the ○○ library. Is ○○ there?

(2) 予約されていた本が用意できました。

The requested book is available.

(3) ○○日までに図書館に取りにいらしてください。

Please come to the library by ○○ and collect the book.

(4) 期間が過ぎると取消しとさせていただきます。

After that date, the reservation will be cancelled.

(5) ご伝言いただけますか？

Could you take a message?

貸出期間延長　　　Renewal

User（U）：今借りている本の貸出を延長したいです。

I'd like to renew a book I have checked out.

Librarian（L）：はい。予約が入っていなければ，1回期間を延長することができます。

All right. If no one else requests it, you can renew it for an additional period.

本をこちらのカウンターに持ってきて手続きしていただけますか。

Bring the book to this counter for renewal.

電話での延長は受け付けられません。

Books cannot be renewed by telephone.

図書館のウェブサイトから延長処理ができます。ログインして手続きをしてください。

The loan period can be extended through library websites. Please log in to the website and proceed with the necessary procedures.

U：何日間この本の貸出を延長できますか？

How long can I renew this book?

L：1週間です。貸出期間内に電話で連絡してください。

One week. Please telephone us before the due date.

L：この本は別の方が予約しているので，残念ですが延長できません。

Another person requested the book. I'm afraid it cannot

72·········Ⅲ　貸出・返却

be renewed.

L：遅れているので延長できません。遅れた場合はこの本が
いったん書架に返却されるまで貸出できません。

It's overdue so it cannot be renewed. When a book is
overdue, it must be returned to the shelf before it can
be checked out again.

L：遅れていても 3 日以内なら延長できます。

If a book is late three days or less, it can be renewed.

L：この本はトカーズ先生のリザーブ図書に指定されました。
今後の貸出は，地下のリザーブ・カウンターでお願いし
ます。

This book is reserved for Prof. Tokarz's class. You can
borrow it from the reserve counter in the basement.

紛失   Lost book

User（U）：借りている資料を，電車の中に置き忘れてしまったのですが，どうすればいいでしょうか？

I forgot a borrowed book on the train. What should I do?

Librarian（L）：駅には届けましたか？

Did you report it at the train station?

U：届けましたが見つかりません。

I did report it but they didn't find it.

L：それはいつですか？

When?

U：先週の日曜日です。

Last Sunday.

L：困りましたね。まず紛失届をご提出ください。しばらく様子を見てどうしても見つからない場合は，同じ資料で弁償していただくことになります。

That's too bad. First you need submit a lost book report. We will wait some time to see if it is returned. If not, you'll have to replace it.

U：同じ資料でないといけませんか？

Does the replacement have to be exactly the same?

L：品切れ，絶版等で買うことができない場合は，値段と扱っている主題が同じものでもかまいません。

If it cannot be purchased because it is out of stock or print, the replacement can be something at the same

　　　　　price for the same subject.
L：現金で弁償していただくことになります。
　　　　　You'll have to pay compensation.
　　取得価格をお支払いいただきます。
　　　　　We'll ask you to pay the acquisition cost.
L：現金でお支払いください。
　　　　　The penalty has to be paid in cash.

督促　　　Follow-up on overdue

Librarian（L）：○○さんのお宅ですか？　こちらは○○図書館です。○○さんはいらっしゃいますか？　ご本人様でいらっしゃいますね。図書館から本を借りていらっしゃいませんでしょうか？　返却期限が過ぎて延滞になっていますので，至急ご返却いただけますか。

> Is this the ○○ residence? I'm with the ○○ library. Is ○○ there? Am I speaking with Mr./Ms.○○? According to our records, you borrowed books from the library, and they are overdue. We'd like it to be returned promptly.

次の予約を入れていらっしゃる方がいます。

> Another user has requested the book and is waiting for it.

いつご返却いただけますか？

> When can you return it?

ではお待ちしています。

> We'll be waiting.

L：お伝えしたいことがあるので，図書館にご連絡くださるようお伝えください。

> Please contact the library as we have something we would like to inform him/her about.

76 ········ Ⅲ　貸出・返却

図書館間相互貸借

Interlibrary loan

図書　　　Books

User（U）：探している図書が図書館にありません。

　　　　　The book I'm searching for isn't in the library.

Librarian（L）：あちらにある端末で調べてみてください。全
国の都道府県立図書館・政令指定都市立図書館の蔵書が
検索できます。もしあればこの図書館に借りてくること
ができます。ただ館外貸出はできません。

　　　　　Try searching on that terminal over there. It searches
for collections from prefectural libraries and libraries
of major cities. If the book is available, this library will
borrow it for you. But, you will not be able to check it
out. You will have to use it in reading room.

L：リクエストサービスで申し込んでください。ご用意できた
ら連絡します。

　　　　　Please apply through the Request Service. We will
contact you when the book is ready.

U：取り寄せるのにどのくらい時間がかかりますか？

　　　　　How much time will the inquiry take?

L：1，2週間かかります。

　　　　　It will take one or two weeks.

U：利用できる期間はどのくらいでしょう？

　　　　　How long will I be able to use it?

L：1か月です。

One month.

U：費用はかかりますか？

Is there a fee?

L：いいえ，かかりません。

No, there is no charge.

User（U）：この図書が○○大学にあると聞いたのですが，取り寄せることができますか？

I was told that this book is at ○○ University. Could you borrow it for me?

Librarian（L）：少しお待ちください。調べてみます。

Please wait a few minutes. I'll check.

たしかに持っていますが，こちらの図書館には貸出をしてくれません。

Yes they do have it, but they will not lend it to our library.

他に△△大学が持っていて，借り出すことができます。

△△ University also has it. They will lend it to us.

U：それはよかった。入手までにどのくらいかかりますか？

That's good. How long will it take until I can get it?

L：確実なことは言えませんが，1週間以内には届くと思います。

I can't say exactly, but I believe it should arrive within a week.

U：費用はかかりますか？

Does it cost anything?

図書·········79

L：はい。実費負担になりますので，先方から請求された金額と，こちらからの返送料，手数料200円をお支払いいただくことになります。

> Yes. You'll have to pay all actual costs, including the amount they bill us, our cost of returning it, and the 200 yen handling charge.

U：どうしても必要なので取り寄せてください。

> I really need it, so please go ahead with it.

L：ではこちらの申込用紙に記入してください。届きましたらご連絡します。

> Please complete this form. We will notify you when it arrives.

User：昨日取り寄せを頼んだものですが，知人で持っている人がいたので，キャンセルしたいです。

> Yesterday I had requested a book from another library, but I found out that a friend of mine has the book, so I'd like to cancel the request.

Librarian：わかりました。先方がまだ発送していなければキャンセルできると思います。連絡してみますのでお待ちいただけますか？

> I understand. If the other library hasn't sent out the item, it can be cancelled. Can you wait while I contact them?

すでに発送済みなのでキャンセルできません。

> They have already sent it out, so we can't cancel it.

雑誌論文　　　Periodical articles

User（U）：もしもし，データベースから出力したリストをお
　　　　送りすれば，記事をいただけますか？

　　　　　Hello. If I send a list from an online database, could
　　　　　you send me copies of the articles?

Librarian（L）：できます。検索結果の希望する文献に印をつ
　　　　けて，メールで送ってください。

　　　　　Yes, we can. Please mark the articles you want and
　　　　　email the list to us.

U：料金はかかりますか？

　　　　　Is there a charge for this?

L：1枚50円の通常料金に加えて，郵送料を払っていただく
　　ことになります。

　　　　　Upon receipt of the material, you will pay a standard
　　　　　fee of 50 yen per page, and for the shipping.

L：リストを送付いただきありがとうございます。残念ですが，
　　この雑誌は購読していません。でも，ILL ネットワーク
　　を使えば取り寄せられます。入手希望ですか？

　　　　　Thank you for sending the list. Unfortunately, we don't
　　　　　subscribe to this periodical. But if we use an interlibrary
　　　　　loan network, we can obtain it. Shall we pursue it?

U：ええ，だけど入手までにどのくらいかかるのでしょう？

　　　　　Yes, but how long will it take to arrive?

雑誌論文………81

L：1 週間くらいかかると思います。

  At least a week.

U：もっと早く入手できませんか？　週末の学会の前に論文が必要です。

  Isn't there a faster way? I have an academic conference on the weekend and want it before that.

L：速達でお送りすることもできます。

  Then we can send the articles by express mail.

U：そうします。

  That's great.

L：費用は，別途，速達料金が必要です。

  Please pay an express mail fee separately.

海外 ILL の利用 　　　International interlibrary loan

User：国内所蔵がない雑誌なのですが，海外からも取り寄せ
　　　は可能ですか？

　　　　　This journal is not held in Japan. Is it possible to
　　　　　borrow journals from overseas libraries?

Librarian：はい，通常は1か月以内に入手できます。

　　　　　Yes, you can usually obtain it within a month.

User：ソルボンヌ大学の学位論文を取り寄せたいのですが。

　　　　　I would like to borrow a doctoral thesis from Sorbonne
　　　　　University.

Librarian：複写するとなると，著者からの許可書が必要にな
　　　ります。

　　　　　If you want it to be photocopied, you must first obtain
　　　　　permission from the author.

　　　場合によっては半年以上かかったり，費用も1万円以上
　　　になるかもしれませんよ。

　　　　　Sometimes, it takes more than six months. Copying
　　　　　may cost more than ten thousand yen.

Librarian：当館では海外からの取り寄せはしていません。こ
　　　の論文は出版社のウェブサイトから論文を直接購入する
　　　ことができます。

Sorry, but we don't handle international interlibrary loan requests. But, papers can be purchased directly from publishers' websites.

V

レファレンス
サービス

Reference service

所蔵調査　　　　Holding check

◆電話での応答　　**Responding to a telephone inquiry**

User（U）：英語の本はおいてありますか？

　　　　　Do you have any books in English?

Librarian（L）：はい，小説と日本を紹介したものなら少しあります。

　　　　　Yes. We have some novels and books introducing Japan.

U：それはよかった。それと *Japan Times* のバックナンバーも見たいです。

　　　　　That's good. I want to also read back issues of the *Japan Times*.

L：レファレンス担当と代わります。

　　　　　I'll connect you with the reference department.

User（U）：日本の楽器について英語で書かれた本がありますか？

　　　　　Do you have any books in English about Japanese musical instruments?

Librarian（L）：はい，あります。

　　　　　Yes, we do.

L：何冊かお求めの主題に関する本があります。

　　　　　We have several books on that topic.

　　例えば『日本音楽と楽器』というタイトルの本があります。

86………Ⅴ　レファレンスサービス

For example, *Japanese Music and Musical Instruments*.

もう1冊,『日本音楽史』というタイトルの本があります。

Another title is *The Music History of Japan*.

その本についてもっとお知りになりたいのでしたら,この本を所蔵している部署／室／係へ電話をお回しします。

If you want to know more about that book, I'll connect your call with the department/room/section that has it.

L：その資料を探すのに少々時間がかかりそうです。

It will take some time to locate that book.

30分／1時間ほどしたら,もう一度電話をかけていただけますか。

Please call back in about 30 minutes/one hour.

それまでにお調べしておきます。

I'll have completed a search by then.

私の名前は岡部と申します。内線は 2552 です。

My name is Okabe. My extension is 2552.

L：残念ながらありません。

No, I'm afraid we don't.

L：ここにはありませんが,○○図書館にはあります。

We don't have the book, but it's at ○○ Library.

U：どうもありがとう。

Thank you.

User（U）：*Journal of Pharmaceutical Methods* を所蔵していますか？

Do you have *Journal of Pharmaceutical Methods*?

所蔵調査········87

Librarian（L）：はい，でも今年度購読を開始したばかりです。

Yes, but our subscription only began this year.

U：かまいません。

That's all right.

L：今日最新号が届きました。

The most recent issue arrived today.

User：日本薬局方は所蔵していますか？

Do you have *Nihon Yakkyokuho*?

Librarian：はい，あります。最新版は 18 版です。ちなみに，厚生労働省のウェブサイトで英文版の日本薬局方を読むことができます。

Yes, we have it. The most recent edition is the eighteenth. For your information, an official English translation is available on the website of the Ministry of Health, Labour and Welfare.

Mr. Williams（U）：すみませんが，本を所蔵しているかお聞きできますか？

Excuse me; I'd like to know if you have a certain book.

Librarian（L）：失礼ですが，ご所属はどちらでしょうか？

Are you affiliated with any institution?/Who is your employer?

U：私は Williams といって，中学校で英語を教えています。

My name is Williams. I teach English in junior high school/middle school.

L：そうですか。特定の本をお探しですか？

I see. Are you searching for a particular book?

U：はい。Rinvolucri の書いた "Grammar Games" という本を探しています。

Yes, I'm searching for a book called *Grammar Games* written by Rinvolucri.

L：著者をもう一度おっしゃってください。

Please state the author's name again.

U：Rinvolucri です。

Rinvolucri.

L：すみませんが，スペルをゆっくり言ってください。

I'm sorry, could you slowly spell it?

U：R.I.N.V.O.L.U.C.R.I., ファーストネームは Mario, M.A.R.I.O. です。

R-I-N-V-O-L-U-C-R-I. The first name is Mario: M-A-R-I-O.

L：繰り返します。R.I.N.B.O.L.U.C.R.I. B は boy の B ですか？

Let me repeat that: R-I-N-B-O-L-U-C-R-I. Is that "B" as in "boy"?

U：いいえ。Victory の V です。

No, "V" as in "victory".

L：失礼しました。ファーストネームは M.A.R.I.O. ですね？

Sorry about that. The first name is M-A-R-I-O. Correct?

U：そうです。

That's right.

L：書名が "Grammar Games" ですね。出版年はいつでしょうか？

The title is *Grammar Games*. When was it published?

U：1984 年に出ていますが，それより新しい版があれば，そ
れでもけっこうです。

> It was first published in 1984, but if there's a newer
> edition, it would be fine.

L：わかりました。今目録を調べます。このまま切らずにお待
ちください。

> I understand. I'll go on and check the catalog. Please
> stay on the line.

お待たせしました。この本は，英語科の研究室に所蔵さ
れています。

> Thank you for waiting. It's in the research collection of
> the English department.

請求記号は PE1128. A2 です。ただし貸出に出ているかど
うかは，こちらではわかりません。

> The call number is PE1128. A2. But I can't verify
> whether it has been checked out.

もし閲覧にいらっしゃるのでしたら，こちらの本館に取
り寄せなければなりませんが，どうしますか？

> If you want to examine it, the main library will obtain
> it for you. What would you like to do?

◆カウンターで　　**Responding at the counter**

User：○○語（英・独・仏・西・中・ハングル等）で書かれ
た本が読みたいです。

> I'd like to read books written in（English, German,
> French, Spanish, Chinese, Korean）.

Librarian（L）：外国語のコーナーがあります。ご案内します

90⋯⋯⋯Ⅴ　レファレンスサービス

ので，一緒にいらしてください。

> We have a foreign language books section. I'll show you where it is. Please follow me.

L：残念ながら○○語の本はありません。

> I'm sorry, we have no books in ○○.

L：○○語の本は，少しですが入っています。OPAC で調べてください。

> We do have some books in ○○. First, please search the OPAC.

L：○○語の本は日本語の本と一緒に配架されています。その主題の棚に行ってみてください。

> Books in ○○ language are shelved together with Japanese books. Please go to the subject's shelves.

User：日本語を学習するための本，CD 等はありますか？

> Do you have any books or CDs for the study of Japanese?

Librarian：ええ，何冊か入っていたと思います。書架に810という数字が入っているところを見てください。

> Yes. There are several books on this topic. Please check on the shelves numbered 810.

それから，視聴覚室に CD があったと思います。

> Additionally, I believe that there are CDs in the audio-visual room.

一緒に蔵書検索で調べてみましょう。これがそうですね。この部分が請求記号です。これがタイトルです。

> I'll help you search the OPAC. Here they are. This is

所蔵調査………91

called the call number. This is the title.

これらをこの用紙に記入して，視聴覚室のカウンターに出してください。

Please complete this form and turn it in at the counter in the audio-visual room.

このアイコンから申し込みができます。申し込んだら視聴覚室に行ってください。

You can apply using this icon. After applying, please visit the audio-visual room.

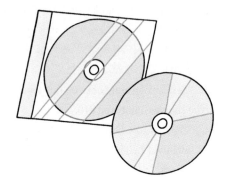

所在調査　　Location search

User（U）：すみません。私は○○大学の学生です。私の大学の図書館で調べてもらって，そちらにあるといわれた雑誌を見たいのですが，必要な号が書架にあるか調べてもらえますか？

Excuse me. I'm a student at ○○ University. The library at my university searched for me and found that your library has a periodical I am searching for. Can you check whether the issue I need is on the shelf?

Librarian：はい。では今電話を雑誌担当のものに代わります。

Yes. I'll connect your call with the periodicals department.

Ms. Kato（K）：お電話代わりました。雑誌担当の加藤です。

Your call has been transferred. This is the periodicals department. Kato speaking.

U：*Journal of Neuropsychology* の 19 巻 2 号を探しています。そちらでお持ちですか？

I need to read the *Journal of Neuropsychology*, Volume 19, Number 2. Do you have it?

K：少々お待ちください。所蔵検索では入っていることになっていますが利用中の場合もあります。

Please hold this line for a moment. According to our catalog, we did receive it, but it may be in use.

所在調査·········93

User：OPAC で調べた本が書架にありません。

A book that was in the catalog is not on the shelf.

Librarian：では貸出中かどうか調べましょう。いいえ，貸出
には出ていませんね。どなたか館内で利用されているか，
返却用のカートの上かもしれません。もうしばらくして
また探してみてください。

Let's check whether it has been checked out. No, it's
not in circulation. Either someone is using it within the
library or it is on a book return cart. Please wait for a
while and then check again.

User：*Economist* の 2020 年 1 月のものが見たいのですが，
書架にありません。

I was searching for a January 2020 issue of the
Economist, but it's not on the shelf.

Librarian（L）：この日付ですと製本に出しているかもしれま
せん。

With that date, it has probably been sent to the bindery.

やはりそうです。来月の 15 日に戻ります。

Yes, that's right. It will return on the fifteenth of the
following month.

L：製本に出すために事務室の方に持ってきています。今お持
ちします。

It's in the office being prepared for the bindery. I'll
obtain it now.

利用がすみましたら，こちらにご返却ください。

Please return it once you have finished reading it.

94………Ⅴ　レファレンスサービス

User：*Drug Design and Delivery* はありますか？

Do you have *Drug Design and Delivery*?

Librarian：所蔵リストをチェックしてみます。はい，所蔵していますが，今年度の号は全然出版されていません。

Let me check the holdings list. Yes, we subscribe, but this year's edition has not yet been published.

User：この雑誌の最新号が書架に見当たらないのですが。

I can't find the current issue of this periodical on the shelf.

Librarian（L）：調べてみましょう。これは終刊です。最終号は 2023 年の 10 巻 4 号です。

Let me check. It has ceased publication. The last issue was Issue 4 of Volume 10 in 2023.

L：この雑誌は 2023 年 1 月号から『○○』という別のタイトルに改題されています。書架を確認してみてください。

This periodical has been retitled under a different title, "○○," since the January 2023 issue. Please check the shelf.

User（U）：『治療』の 7 月号が見当たりません。

I can't find the July issue of *Chiryo*.

Librarian（L）：チェックしてみましょう。もう受入れしています。どなたかが利用されているか，無断で研究室へ持って行かれたのかもしれません。困っています。

Let's check. We've received it. Someone is reading it or it has been taken to the study room without checking it

　　　　　out. It is a problem.
U：困りましたね。
　　　　　It sure is.
L：戻りましたら電話でお知らせします。
　　　　　We will contact you, once it has been returned.
　　内線は何番ですか？
　　　　　What is your extension?
U：560 です。
　　　　　Five-six-zero.

事項調査　　　Fact Search

User（U）:「なまこ壁」というのがなぜ「なまこ」というのか，どのように調べたらいいですか？

　　　　I'd like to find out why sea cucumber walls are called that.

Librarian（L）: 英語で日本を紹介している *Encyclopedia of Japan* は調べましたか？

　　　　Did you search in the *Encyclopedia of Japan*, which introduces Japan in English?

　　データベースのジャパンナレッジは検索されましたか？

　　　　Did you search the database called "JapanKnowledge"?

U:ええ，でも私にはあの白い部分がなまこに見えるのかわかりません。

　　　　Yes, I don't understand why the white part looks like a sea cucumber.

L:そうですか，私にもすぐには説明できません。少しお時間をいただいて，日本語の文献をお調べすることはできます。

　　　　Oh, well, just off-hand, I can't explain it either. If you can wait for a while, I'll search in the Japanese language sources.

U:できたらお願いします。建築関係の記事を書いているので，できたら1週間くらいでわかれば嬉しいです。

　　　　Yes, please if you can. I'm writing an article about

事項調査⋯⋯⋯97

architecture, and I'd like to receive the the information within a week or so.

L：確実に満足のいく調査ができるかどうかわかりませんが，やってみます。

I don't know if I'll be able to find a satisfactory explanation, but I'll try.

こちらにご連絡先を記入してください。

Please write down where you can be contacted.

利用案内　　Access to materials

◆単行本の分類法　　**Classification of monographs**

User（U）：この図書館の分類法について教えてください。

Please tell me about the classification system you use at this library.

Librarian（L）：この図書館では本を主題から探す手立てとして，日本十進分類法（NDC）を採用しています。

In this library, books are arranged by subject according to the Nippon Decimal Classification（NDC）.

NDC は，主題を数字に換える法則です。この分類表を見てください。

Within the NDC, the subjects are represented by numbers. Check this copy of the classification system.

U：正式な書名と著者名がわからないのですが，どのように探せばよいでしょう？

I don't know the exact title or author, so how do I search?

L：分類体系があります。

It depends on the classification system.

外国語図書は NLM（米国立医学図書館）の分類法です。

Foreign language books are in the National Library of Medicine Classification（NLMC）.

日本語図書は NDC で分類しています。

Japanese books are in NDC.

利用案内·········99

分類表は，あちらの壁に掲示してあります。

> The classification system is displayed on the wall over there.

L：収書の範囲が狭いので，独自の分類をしています。

> We collect books in a narrow range and have our own classification system.

何について書かれた本をお探しですか？

> What is the subject of the book you are searching for?

私の方で分類番号をお調べします。

> I'll find out the classification number.

User（U）：日本文学に関して英語で書かれた本を見たいです。

> I want to read books in English about Japanese literature.

Librarian（L）：日本文学に関する本をお探しですか？ この図書館で採用しているこの日本十進分類法を見てください。日本文学は 910 という分類番号が与えられていますね。外国語図書の分類番号で 910 番台の書架を見れば，英語で書かれた図書が見つかると思います。

> If you are searching for books in Japanese literature, understand the Nippon Decimal Classification system used by this library. Under this system, Japanese literature is assigned the classification number 910. In the classified catalog for foreign language books, shelves beginning with 910 should include those written in English.

L：日本文学といっても漠然としていますね。どのような文献をお探しですか？

Japanese literature is a broad topic. More specifically, what sort of literature are you looking for?

U：短歌について知りたいのです。

I want to know about *tanka*.

L：それでしたら OPAC で NDC に 911 という番号を入れてお調べください。

In this case, please input the number 911 into the NDC on the OPAC.

U：どうやって調べればいいですか？

How do I search?

L：OPAC のプルダウンから NDC を選んでください。そこに 911 と入力して，検索ボタンをクリックしてください。

Please select the NDC from the pull-down menu of OPAC, input 911, and click the search button.

◆ OPAC の利用方法　　**OPAC use**

Librarian（L）：当館の蔵書は，OPAC で調べることができます。

You can check our library's holdings on the OPAC.

L：これがトップ画面です。

Here is the top page.

ここに調べたい言葉を入力します。

Enter your search terms here.

詳細検索画面もあります。ここをクリックしてください。

An advanced search is also available. Click here.

英語を入力する場合は，「半角／全角」キーを押してからタイプしてください。

If you want to enter English words, press the key with

利用案内⋯⋯⋯101

the characters "Half-width/Full-width" and then type.

L：この言葉でヒットする文献が複数ある場合は，該当文献が一覧表示されます。

When multiple items have your search terms, a list of the relevant items is displayed.

検索結果の一覧から選んでクリックすると，詳細表示に変わります。

If you select one and click on an item on the list, a screen showing details about that item appears.

並べ替えたり絞り込んだりすることができます。

And, the results can be sorted or limited.

データの最後に所蔵情報が付いています。

The location information is at the end of the data.

これが請求記号，配置場所，これが現在の状態です。空欄なので，書架にあるはずです。探してみてください。

Here is the call number and the location where it is shelved. This is its status now. It is on the shelf, hence, please search for it on the stacks.

L：地下書庫にある本の利用申込もこの OPAC から行うことができます。図書館利用者カードを読み込んで，申込ボタンをクリックしてください。他の方が利用中の場合には，予約ボタンをクリックしてください。これで予約終了です。

You can apply for the use of the book in basement stacks on OPAC. Please load your library card and click on "Apply." If another person uses the book, click on "Reserve." This concludes the reservation process.

102········Ⅴ レファレンスサービス

L：OPAC の画面右上に言語の切替えボタンがあります。英語，中国語，韓国語を選択できます。

> A key in the upper-right corner of OPAC switches the language. English, Chinese, and Korean languages can be selected.

ヘルプ機能も各言語で表示されますから，ご自分で実際に使ってみてください。

> This help function displays information in different languages. Try it yourself.

探している本が見つからない場合には，図書館員にお尋ねください。

> If you can't find your desired book, please ask the librarians.

《質問例　図書の検索　　Example question: Searching for monographs》

User（U）：『マクロエコノミクス』という書名の本を探しています。

> I'm searching for a book called *Macroeconomics*.

Librarian（L）：OPAC で調べましたか？

> Did you search in the OPAC?

U：はい。でも件数が多すぎてうまく探せません。

> Yes, but there were too many hits. I couldn't find what I wanted.

L：著者はわかりますか？

> Do you know the author?

U：フランス人のブランシャールという人です。

利用案内········103

A French named Blanchard.

L：スペルとファーストネームはわかりますか？

What is the spelling of the author's name, and what is the first name?

U：B.l.a.n.c.h.a.r.d だと思います。でも後はよくわかりません。

B-l-a-n-c-h-a-r-d. I don't know the first name.

L：そうですか。出版年か，出版社名はわかりますか？

Do you know the year of publication or the publisher's name?

U：いいえ，でもそんなに古くないと思います。ここ 3 ～ 5 年以内の出版だと思います。

No, but it's not that old. I believe it has been published in the last three to five years.

L：ではインターネットで出版情報を確認してみます。

OK, I'll check the internet for publication information.

これですね。著者は Olivier Blanchard です。出版年が 2021 年，Pearson から出ています。

Here it is. The author is Olivier Blanchard. The publication year is 2021 and it is from Pearson.

これらの情報で絞り込んでみるとよいと思います。

You can narrow your search using this information.

L：比較的書名に使われる言葉ですからね。もし書名が確かなら，完全一致検索というものができます。書名の後に「／」記号をつけて検索してください。

It is a word frequently used in titles. If you are certain that the title is the entire title, then we can perform an exact-match search. After inputting the title, add a slash

104⋯⋯⋯Ⅴ　レファレンスサービス

"/", then search again.

《質問例　OPAC 件名　Example question: Subject searching of the OPAC》

User：歌舞伎について書かれた本を探しています。

I'm searching for books about *kabuki*.

Librarian：OPAC で調べましたか？

Did you search in the OPAC?

件名のところに「歌舞伎」と入れてみてください。

Input *kabuki* as a subject and search.

あるいは，この件名標目表にある関連の言葉を入れて調べてみてください。

Or else select related words from this list of subject headings and use them for the search.

◆レファレンスブック案内　Reference books

(1) 日本関係欧文図書目録はこちらです。

The catalog for western books related to Japan is here.

(2) そのテーマで文献をお探しなら，いくつか書誌をご紹介しましょう。

For information on that topic, I can recommend several bibliographies.

(3) 巻頭に凡例が出ていますが，これが著者，論題，雑誌名，掲載巻号，刊行年月日，掲載ページです。

An explanation is provided at the beginning of the volume: It shows that this is the author, article title, periodical title, volume number, publication date, and page.

利用案内⋯⋯⋯105

(4)　雑誌名は省略されていますから，巻末の対照表を調べて
　ください。

> The periodical title is abbreviated, so refer to the list at the
> back of the volume.

(5)　文献の配列はこの書誌独自の分類によります。

> This bibliography uses its own classification to place the
> items in order.

(6)　1990 年以降 2000 年までは CD-ROM で刊行，それ以降は
　インターネット公開されています。

> From 1990 until 2000, it was published on CD-ROM, and
> since then it has been available on the internet.

《質問例　人物情報　　**Example question: Biographical information**》

User（U）：国連で活躍している，あるいは活躍した日本人に
　ついて知りたいです。

> I want to search about the Japanese who are or were
> active in the United Nations.

Librarian（L）：特定の人物をお調べですか？

> Anyone in particular?

U：いいえ，どんな人がいるのかもよくわかりません。

> No, I don't know who is involved.

L：日本語でもよろしいでしょうか？

> Is information in Japanese all right?

U：私は読めませんが，友人が訳してくれると思います。

> I can't read it, but a friend will translate it for me.

L：では，英語の文献から調べてみましょう。

106………Ⅴ　レファレンスサービス

First let's examine the sources in English.

《**質問例　団体情報**　**Example question: Information about organizations**》

User（U）：Japan Society for Studies in Journalism and Mass Communication という団体があるそうなのですが，連絡先のメールアドレスを知りたいです。

> I'd like to obtain the email address of the Japan Society for Studies in Journalism and Mass Communication.

Librarian：英語で書かれたディレクトリーはないので，日本語のもので調べてみましょう。

> We don't have an English language directory. I'll search in the Japanese directory.

現在は，日本メディア学会という名称に変わっているようです。

> It appears that the name has now been changed to Japan Association for Media, Journalism and Communication Studies.

学会のウェブサイトがありました。一部のページには英文が併記されているようです。

> This is the website of the Association: Some pages have been written in English.

学会のウェブサイトの URL をお書きしましょうか？

> Shall I write down the URL of the Association for you?

U：お願いします。

> Please.

利用案内⋯⋯⋯107

《質問例　統計　**Example question: Statistics**》

User（U）：日本の製造業の海外直接投資について知りたいです。

I'd like to find out about foreign investment by Japanese manufacturers.

Librarian（L）：文献をお探しですか，それともデータが必要ですか？

Are you looking for books and articles or data?

U：データがまず必要です。特に業種別の投資額が知りたいのです。会社別のデータがあればベストです。他に政府刊行物や雑誌の文献があればそれも読みたいのです。

First I need data. The amounts are based on the type of industry. The best would be the data provided by the company. In addition, I'd like to examine government publications and periodical articles, if any.

L：でしたらまず, 統計のコーナーにある『財政金融統計月報』の「対内外民間投資特集」の号を見るといいでしょう。

First let's look at the issue of Special Feature on Inward and Outward Private Investment of *Ministry of Finance Statistics Monthly* in our statistics section.

ただ会社別のデータは載っていないかもしれません。

I don't recall any data provided by the company.

一緒に行って調べましょう。こちらへどうぞ。

Let's go and I'll help you search. This way.

L：では，そのデータが何に載っているか，国立国会図書館の「リサーチ・ナビ」を使って調べてみます。

To determine where the data are, I'll use "Research

108········Ⅴ　レファレンスサービス

Navi" provided by the National Diet Library.

しばらくお待ちください。

Please wait for a few minutes.

L：では，統計資料室に行って調べてください。専任の係のものがいます。

You should perform that search in the statistical materials room. Staff will be there to help.

◆他館の紹介　**Introductions to other libraries**

User（U）：最近の日本の SF 小説で英訳されたものを読みたいです。

I'd like to read a recent Japanese science fiction novel in translation.

Librarian（L）：この図書館には残念ながら，現代文学作品やその英訳は集めていません。

Unfortunately, this library doesn't collect modern literature or its translations.

大きな公共図書館では持っていると思います。

I believe a large public library may have them.

U：どこで持っているかわかりますか？

Do you know which library?

L：○○図書館あたりでしょうか。特にどの作家が読みたいというわけではありませんか？

It may be held at the ○○ Library. Is there any particular author that you want to read?

U：どんな作家がいるのかも知りません。

I don't know any authors.

さっき言っていた図書館は遠いですか？

Is the library you mentioned far?

L：いいえ，そんなには遠くありません。1時間くらいで行けます。

No, not very far. You could reach in an hour.

U：じゃあ，行ってみます。どう行けばいいですか？

Well, I'll visit it. How do I reach there?

L：○○図書館は開架資料が多いので，そちらを紹介します。

○○ Library has many open stacks. I recommend you to visit it.

念のため○○図書館に行く前に，電話で問い合わせた方がよいと思います。

Before visiting ○○ library, I suggest you call the library.

U：近くで持っていそうなところはありますか？

Is there any place nearby that is likely to provide such books?

L：では，近くの図書館の目録を調べてみます。

I'll check the holdings at a nearby library.

L：「国立国会図書館サーチ」というウェブサイトで，都道府県立図書館や政令指定都市立図書館などの所蔵資料を検索することができます。

You can search for materials held by prefectural libraries and libraries of major cities by using the website: NDL Search.

全国の7,400以上の図書館の所蔵や貸出状況を検索できる「カーリル」というサービスもあります。

Moreover, a service called "Calil" allows users to search the holdings and borrowing status of more than 7,400 libraries nationwide.

U：取り寄せはできますか？

Could you have the book(s) sent here?

L：国立国会図書館からは取り寄せられます。

The National Diet Library will send books to us.

ただし，取り寄せとなると特定の資料でないとできませんし，送料は負担していただきます。

But we have to request specific titles. You'll have to pay the postage costs.

それでよろしければ，申込方法について詳しくご説明します。

If this is acceptable, we'll explain the application process in detail.

オンラインリソース　　Online resource

◆国立国会図書館デジタル化資料送信サービス
The Digitized Contents Transmission Service

User：こちらの図書館で国立国会図書館の図書館向けデジタル化資料送信サービスは使えますか。

Do you provide the Digitized Contents Transmission Service for Libraries?

Librarian (L)：はい，カウンター前の端末を使って，利用することが可能です。

Yes, you can use the service on the computer in front of the counter.

L：申し訳ありませんが，当館は参加館ではないため，利用することができません。ただし，個人向けデジタル化資料送信サービス（個人送信）を利用して閲覧することもできます。

We apologize that our library is not a partner library, so we can't provide the service. The Digitized Contents Transmission Service for Individuals is available to the general public via the internet.

◆データベース，電子ジャーナルなど　　**Online search**

User：卒業論文に必要な文献を調べたいのですが，どのデータベースを使えばいいかわかりません。

I want to collect documents necessary for senior theses,

112·········Ⅴ　レファレンスサービス

but I don't know which online database to use.

Librarian：はい，レファレンスデスクへ行ってください。

> Yes. Please go to the reference desk/section.

レファレンス担当にご相談ください。

> Please ask the reference librarian.

図書館ではいろいろなデータベースを契約していますので，レファレンス担当がご質問に最も適切なデータベースをお伝えいたします。

> Our library subscribes to various databases, so the reference librarian will select the most appropriate database for the topic.

User：医中誌 Web の使い方を教えてください。

> Please tell me how to search the Ichushi-Web.

Librarian：有料データベースから検索することができます。利用者用の端末の壁にデータベースの使い方案内等を置いてあります。ご質問があれば，遠慮なくおたずねください。

> You can search in the fee-based databases. Information about how to use the databases is available on the walls of the terminal. If you have any questions, please feel free to ask us.

User（U）：他にどのようなデータベースや電子ジャーナルがありますか？

> Are there any online databases or e-journals that I can search for?

オンラインリソース………113

Librarian（L）：はい。大学図書館ウェブサイトに，電子ジャーナル・データベース一覧のページがあります。

　　　　　　Yes. Our University Library website contains a list of e-journals and databases.

U：自宅からもデータベースを使うことはできますか？

　　　　　　Can I use the online database from home?

L：はい。VPN 経由で利用することができます。

　　　　　　Yes, you can use online databases via VPN.

L：いいえ。図書館内でしか利用することはできません。

　　　　　　No, you can only use the online databases within the library.

《質問例　電子ジャーナル　　Example question: E-journal》

User（U）：医学関連の英語の論文を調べたいのですが，どうやって調べればいいですか？

　　　　　　I'd like to search for medicine-related articles in English. How can I research?

Librarian（L）：PubMed を使ってはいかがでしょうか？

　　　　　　How about using PubMed?

U：自分で調べられますか？

　　　　　　Can I search by myself?

L：はい。疾患名や医学用語，薬品名などのキーワード，雑誌名などから論文を検索することができます。MeSH というシソーラスを使って検索すると，検索漏れやノイズの減少につながるので，試してみてください。

　　　　　　Yes, you can search for articles using keywords, such as a disease, medical term, drug name, and journal. Try

114········Ⅴ　レファレンスサービス

using a thesaurus called MeSH to help reduce search omissions and noise.

U：プリントアウトはできますか？

Can I obtain a printout?

L：はい，できます。Format で Summary 形式の表示等に変更し，ブラウザの印刷メニューをご利用ください。表示を変更せずに印刷すると，不必要な枠・画像が印刷されますのでご注意ください。事前にレコード番号脇のボックスにチェックを入れてから表示を変更すると，チェックしたデータのみが変更した形式で表示されます。

Yes, you can. Please change the display to Summary in Format and use your browser's Print menu. Please note that unnecessary frames and images will be printed if you print without changing the display. If you change the display after checking the boxes by the record number in advance, only the checked data will be displayed in the changed format.

User：論文のフルテキストを見るにはどうすればいいですか？

How can I obtain the full text article?

Librarian（L）：フルテキストへのリンクというボタンがあるので，そこから見ることができます。

Click "Full text" to view the article.

L：フルテキストへのリンクがないので，冊子体の雑誌を持っているか当館の OPAC で検索してみてください。もし所蔵していなければ，国立国会図書館や他の大学図書館の

オンラインリソース………115

所蔵状況を調べる必要があります。

> This article doesn't include the link of "Full text," so, please check the holdings of the journal by our library's OPAC. If we don't hold it, you will need to check the holdings at the National Diet Library or other university libraries.

L：電子ジャーナルの収録対象が 1999 年以降なので，それより前の論文は収録されていません。

> E-journals are only available from 1999 onward; so articles from earlier years are not included.

◆ SDI サービス　　**SDI service**

User：このテーマの新着資料の情報を得るにはどうすればいいですか？

> How can I obtain information on new materials on this subject?

Librarian：はい，登録したキーワードに合う新着資料が図書館に入ると，メールでお知らせする SDI サービスがあります。新着資料が図書館に入った場合，毎週月曜日の午前 10 時にメールでお知らせします。図書館のマイページからキーワードを登録することができます。

> Yes, the SDI service notifies you by email when new arrivals matching your registered keywords enter the library. You will be notified by email every Monday at 10:00 a.m. You can register your keywords on the library's My Page.

◆検索講習会　**Searching workshops**

User：図書館では，OPAC やデータベース等の使い方の講習
　　　会をやっていますか？

　　　　　　　Does the library offer training courses on how to use
　　　　　　　OPAC, databases, and so on?

Librarian（L）：ええ。入口に予定をお知らせしてあります。
　　　図書館のウェブサイトや SNS でもお知らせしています。

　　　　　　　Yes, it does. Schedules are posted at the entrance. This
　　　　　　　information is also available on the library's website
　　　　　　　and social networking sites.

L：ええっと，次は 10 月 15 日に 2 階のセミナールームで開催
　　されますね。

　　　　　　　Let me see. The next session will be held in the seminar
　　　　　　　room on the second floor on October 15.

L：ドアのところに，次回のオンライン検索セミナーについて
　　貼ってあります。申込みは，図書館のウェブサイトから
　　お願いします。

　　　　　　　The notice about the next online seminar is on the door.
　　　　　　　Please apply via the library website.

《質問例　インターネット　**Example question: Internet**》

User（U）：インターネットで検索をしたいです。

　　　　　　　I want to search the internet.

Librarian（L）：専用端末でお申し込みください。利用時間は
　　1 回 30 分までです。ただし，次に予約がない場合は，1
　　回だけ延長することができます。延長を希望される場合
　　は，利用時間終了前までに，カウンターで延長手続きを

オンラインリソース………117

してください。

> Please register at the dedicated terminal. You can use the service for up to 30 minutes at a time. But, if there are no subsequent bookings, you can extend the time only once. If you wish to extend your time, please apply for an extension at the counter before the end of the usage time.

U：Google アカウントにログインできないのですが。

> I can't log in to my Google account.

L：ID，パスワードを入力して特定の個人のみ利用できるサイトは利用することができません。

> It is not possible to use websites where IDs and passwords are available only to certain individuals.

ゲームや SNS への書き込みなどはできません。

> It is not possible to play games or post on social networking sites.

U：検索結果を印刷するか，USB にコピーすることはできますか？

> Can the search results be printed or copied to a USB?

L：印刷やコピーはできません。閲覧のみです。なお，画面の写真撮影もできません。

> Printing and photocopying are not permitted. Only viewing is permitted. You can't take a photo of the screen either.

研究者向けサービス　　Services for scholars

◆雑誌の投稿規定　　**Rules for submitting an article to a journal**

User：*Journal of Toxicology and Environmental Health* の投稿規定を知りたいです。

I'd like to understand the contribution rules of the *Journal of Toxicology and Environmental Health.*

Librarian：この雑誌は現在購読していますので，Instructions for Authors の載っているページを見てください。

As we currently subscribe to this journal, search for the page describing the Instructions for Authors.

Librarian：当方では貴誌＿＿＿＿＿＿＿＿に投稿（寄稿）したいと存じます。投稿規定または投稿に関する諸用紙類をお送りください。

One of the researchers of our institute would like to submit the paper on ＿＿＿＿＿＿（研究課題）to your journal ＿＿＿＿＿＿（誌名）. Please send us the directions or rules for contributing to your journal, as we have been unable to find such information in your published journals.

◆特許情報調査　　**Patent information searches**

User：特定主題の特許情報を探しています。どうやって探し

研究者向けサービス………119

たらよいか教えてください。

> I'd like to search for patent information on a particular subject. Please tell me how to find it.

Librarian：日本の情報を探しているのでしたら，「特許情報プラットフォーム（J-PlatPat)」で調べることができます。各種キーワード，分類，発明者，出願人などから特許・実用新案などを検索できます。外国の情報を探しているのでしたら，「Espacenet」や「Patent Public Search」などをお勧めします。

> Well, if you are searching for information on Japan, you can use the Japan platform for patent information called "J-PlatPat". Patents and utility models can be searched for using various keywords, classifications, inventors, and applicants. If you are searching for information on foreign countries, we recommend using "Espacenet" or "Patent Public Search".

VI

館内案内

Information and announcement

サイン，各種表示，催し物案内
Signs, notices, special events

(1)　10月20日から11月2日まで，蔵書点検のため閉館いたします。

　　From October 20 to November 2, the library will remain closed for inventory purposes.

(2)　8月10日から8月18日まで，夏期休暇期間中につき開館時間を変更いたします。

　　From August 10 to August 18, the library service hours will change to the summer vacation schedule.

(3)　3月7日，地下AVホールにて，○○先生の講演会を行います。

　　March 7, Prof. ○○ will lecture in the basement audio-visual hall.

(4)　視聴覚ホールにて，映画上映会を行います。

　　The film will be shown in the audio-visual hall.

(5)　展示会は，入場無料で6月17日から10月4日まで開催します。

　　The exhibition is free to enter and will run from June 17 to October 4.

(6)　図書館内の忘れ物は，1階カウンターで保管しています。

　　Personal possessions forgotten in the library will be held at the first floor counter.

(7)　資料の貸出を利用される方は，返却期限をお守りくださ

い。

Those who check out library materials are asked to observe the due dates.

(8)　返却の遅れは他の利用者のご迷惑になります。

Delayed return will cause inconvenience to other users.

(9)　図書の又貸しは禁止事項です。返却の遅延，紛失の原因となりますので，やめてください。

Borrowing books and passing them to another person is forbidden. This leads to overdues and the loss of books. Please could you stop it.

館内放送　　　Announcement

(1)　○○さん／○○番でお待ちの方，頼まれた図書が利用で
　　きるようになりました。図書カウンターまでお越しくださ
　　い。

　　　　　＿＿＿＿＿ : The requested book is available. Please come to
　　the book counter.

(2)　○○さん／○○番でお待ちの方，コピーができあがりま
　　した。複写カウンターまでお越しください。

　　　　　＿＿＿＿＿ : The copy you requested is ready. Please come to
　　the photocopying counter.

(3)　貸出カウンターは 19 時 30 分で終了します。貸出を希望
　　される方はお早めにカウンターまでお越しください。

　　　　The circulation counter closes at 19:30. Please come early to
　　the counter before that to borrow a book.

(4)　まもなく閉館の時間です。お忘れ物のないよう，気をつ
　　けてお帰りください。

　　　　The library will be closing soon. Please take care not to
　　forget anything.

(5)　（雑誌名／書名）を無断で持ち出された方は，至急返却
　　してください。

　　　　Attention. The patron uses (periodical title/book title)
　　without checking out, please return it immediately.

(6)　お車の移動をお願いします。湘南ナンバー○○○○，白
　　のプリウスでお越しのお客様は至急お車を移動してくださ

124………Ⅵ　館内案内

い。繰り返します。湘南ナンバー〇〇〇〇，白のプリウスでお越しのお客様は至急お車を移動してください。

Attention: Driver of a white Prius with the license number Shonan 〇〇〇〇: please move your car. I repeat. Driver of a white Prius with the license number Shonan 〇〇〇〇: please move your car.

(7) 館内の皆様に迷子のご案内をいたします。黄色のTシャツにジーンズをはいた3歳くらいの女の子をお預かりしております。お心当たりの方は，1階受付カウンターまでお越しください。

Attention Please.

If you have lost a girl of about three years old wearing a yellow t-shirt and jeans, please collect her from the reception counter on the first floor. We have found her.

(8) 館内の皆様にご案内します。本日午後2時から，3階ラウンジにて，データベース講習会を開催します。予約は不要です。参加をご希望の方は，直接3階ラウンジまでお越しください。

Attention Please.

A database workshop will be held today at 2:00 p.m. in the 3rd floor lounge. Reservations are not required. If you wish to attend, please come directly to the third floor lounge.

付録

Appendix

1. 寄贈

(1) 寄贈依頼のサンプル

拝啓 _____博士殿

    Dear Dr._____

博士が著者の1人（編集者）となっていらっしゃいます
_____というタイトルの出版物を1部いただけ
るかどうかおうかがいします。

    We are writing to inquire about receiving a copy of the publi-
    cation titled _____ of which you are one of the authors
    (editors).

私たちはその出版物に関心がありますので，1部いただけれ
ばたいへんありがたく思います。

    We are interested in this publication. We would appreciate it if
    you could send us a copy.

敬具

    Yours sincerely,

（署名）

田中泰夫

B大学図書館

東京都中央区新川■-◇-○

    Yasuo Tanaka

B University Library

■ - ◇ - ○ Shinkawa, Chuo-ku, Tokyo, Japan

Phone +81-3- ○○○○ - △△△△ (direct line)

E-mail address・・・・・@・・・・

(2) 雑誌の寄贈依頼の簡単なサンプル

貴学／学会／協会で出版された次の（下記の）雑誌を当方の図書館に寄贈していただきたいと存じます。

We would like to have the following journal, published by your university/academic society/association, in our library.

（誌名）＿＿＿＿＿＿＿＿＿＿＿＿＿＿＿＿＿＿＿＿＿

ご承諾のご返事をいただけるのをお待ちしています。

We look forward to your response.

受領書と礼状

図書館名，住所

RECEIPT

Date:

Dear

We acknowledge the receipt of the ＿＿＿＿＿＿＿＿

Yours sincerely,

（署名）

（図書館名）

(3) 日本語・英語兼用の受領書

RECEIPT
受領書

To:

Ref. No. 参照番号
Date 受領日

This is to acknowledge the receipt of the following:
（下記の資料を受領しました）

_____

Institution/Affiliation（機関名／所属機関名）
Specialty（専門分野）
Address（住所）

Name & Signature（貴名および署名または捺印）

(4) 交換依頼とその礼状

貴学で出版されている＿＿＿＿＿＿＿＿＿という雑誌を，
交換雑誌としてお送りいただけませんでしょうか。お送りい
ただければ，当方の大学の研究所で発行しています＿＿＿＿
＿＿＿＿＿の 2000 年 8 巻 1 号から送付することができま
す。バックナンバーもお申込いただければお送りできます。

Dear Sir:
We would like to receive the Journal of ＿＿ published by

your university on an exchange basis. If you send us this journal, we can send the Journal of _____ issued by the Institute of our university, beginning with the first issue of Volume 8, 2000. Back issues will be available upon request.

Sincerely,

貴学の雑誌_____を交換雑誌としてご送付を決めていただき感謝しております。当方では_____を 8 巻 1 号から送付開始します。
今後ともよろしくお願い申し上げます。重ねてお礼を申し上げます。

We appreciate your decision to send the _____ of your university on an exchange basis. We will send you our journal _____ from Volume 8, Number 1.
We expect that this cooperation will continue.
Thank you again.

（5）住所変更
2025 年……日付けで当方は図書館（事務所／会社／研究所）を下記の住所に移転します。
新住所：
今後_____を上記の住所に送付してください。
　　As of ……（日付）, 2025, the address of this library（office/firm/institution）will change to:

付録………131

New address:
Please send _____ hereafter to the new address.
Thank you.

(6) 宛名訂正

当方では雑誌_____を購読しておりますが，宛先が違っていますので，下記の住所に訂正してください。

We have been subscribing to your journal _____,
but our address on the label is incorrect. Please correct the
address as follows:

2. クレーム処理

次の出版物をまだ受け取っていません。

We have not received the following publication yet.

次の単行本をまだ受け取っていません。

We have not received the book _____.

添付した請求書のコピーを参照して至急購読開始してください。早急にお願いします。

Please refer to the attached copy of the invoice and begin our
subscription at once. Thank you for your prompt response.

欠号分を送ってください。

Please replace the missing issue (s).

Please send replacements for the missing issues.

2023 年 9 巻 12 号をまだ受領していません。

We have failed to receive: Vol.9 No.12, 2023.

お送りくださいますようお願いします。

We should appreciate your supplying it.

代理店を通じて購読している雑誌 A の次の号が届いていません。

The following issue of Journal A, subscribed through our agent, has not been received so far.

至急に送付方よろしく。

Please supply it at the earliest.

発送済みの場合には，この通知を無視してください。

Please ignore this if you have already dispatched the same.

雑誌 B 4 巻 4 号を受け取りましたが，10 ページから 20 ページまで落丁しています。

We have received Journal B, Vol.4 No.4, and find that pages 10 to 20 are missing.

印刷状態が悪い。

Printing is defective（poor）.

乱丁があります。

Non-consecutive numbering appears.

Erratic pagination is observed.

10 ページから 20 ページまで白紙です。

Blank pages appear from 10 to 20.

我々の雑誌 D との交換で雑誌 C を送付していただいてありがとうございます。

_____（クレーム内容）。できるだけ早くお

送りいただければありがたく存じます。

Thank you for sending us Journal C in exchange for Journal D. _____ （クレーム内容）. We would appreciate it if you sent this issue at your earliest convenience.

12月9日にお願いした文献複写をいただきましたが，ミスコピーでした。再度以下の論文を複写してください。

We received the photocopy we requested on December 9. But we found that it was miscopied. Please photocopy and resend the following article once again.

雑誌名　　　　　　巻号　　　　　　年　　　　　　ページ
著者名　　　　　　　　　　　　論文名
Journal of A　Vol.　No.　Year　p
Author　　　　Title

お手を煩わせてすみません。

We apologize for the inconvenience.

よろしくお願いします。

Regards,

（当図書館では）東京の取次店を通じてそちらの雑誌を購読していますが，今日まで下記の号が届いていません。

Journal of Clinical and Laboratory Immunology

　　　27巻から29巻（2019）索引

　　　30巻（2020）から31巻の全号

　　　34巻以降全号

そちらの雑誌は我々の研究にとって非常に重要なものです。できるだけ早く補充を下記の住所あて送付くださるようお願

いします。

早急のご返事をお待ちしています。

よろしくお願いします。

Dear Sir:

We have been subscribing to your journal through our agent
（国内取次店名）, Tokyo, Japan.

To date, we have not received the following issues.

Journal of Clinical and Laboratory Immunology

　　Vol.27 to 29（2019）index

　　Vol.30（2020）to 31 all numbers

　　Vol.34（2024）No.1 and thereafter.

Your journal is important for this research. We would appreciate
your sending the replacement copies to the following address
as soon as possible.

　　（自館の住所，宛名）

We look forward to hearing from you soon. Thank you.

Sincerely,

3. 国立国会図書館東京本館　利用案内「Quick guide」

入館　　**When visiting the National Diet Library（NDL）**

　国立国会図書館への利用者用入口は，図書館の東側にあり
ます。図書は国立国会図書館本館，雑誌は新館でご覧いただ
けます。本館と新館は連絡通路で結ばれています。（入口の位
置は国立国会図書館の館内案内図をご覧ください。）利用者登

録をしていない方は，新館入口からご入館ください。

> The visitors' entrance to the NDL is on its eastern side. Books are available in the NDL Main Building, and Periodicals in the Annex. The Main Building and the Annex are linked by corridors.（See the Map of the National Diet Library for the entrance location.）Non-registered users must enter the Library from the entrance in the Annex.

セキュリティ等の理由により，以下のものは図書館内に持ち込めません。エントランスホールのロッカーに入れてください。（ロッカーを利用するには 100 円硬貨を入れる必要があります。再度ロッカーを開けると硬貨が戻ってきます。）財布や筆記具，貴重品はロッカールームに備え付けのリユース袋に入れてお持ちください。

> For security and other reasons, the following cannot be brought into the Library. Please put these items in the lockers in the entrance hall.（To use a locker, you need to put in a 100-yen coin. The coin will be returned when you open the locker again.）You can take your purse, writing instruments, and valuables with you in a transparent bag provided in the Locker Room.

カードをタッチしてゲートを通り，ご入館ください。

> To open the Entrance Gate and enter, registered users touch the user card on the Gate.

まだ登録されていない方は，新館の利用者登録カウンターで利用者登録をし，カードを受け取ることができます。

> If you have not already registered, you can apply for user registration and receive a Registration Card at User Registration

136………付録

Counter in the Annex.

※　憲政資料室，古典籍資料室，音楽・映像資料室の利用には許可が必要です。

※　図書館では，資料の受け取りや複写申込書に記入するために筆記具が必要です。また，複写料金も必要です。

※　図書館のサービスや資料に関する詳しい情報は，本館・新館インフォメーションまでお問い合わせください。

* Permission is required to use the Modern Japanese Political History Materials Room, the Rare Books and Old Materials Room, and the Music and Audio-Visual Materials Room.

* In the Library, you will need a writing instrument to fill in forms to receive materials or have them photocopied. You will also need some money with you to pay for photocopy services.

* For more information about the Library's services and materials, please inquire at the General Information Desk in the Main Building and Annex.

利用者登録をせずに入館を希望される方は，「当日利用カード」を取得できます。

Users wishing to enter without making a user registration can obtain a One Day User Card.

図書館の端末を利用して資料の検索，請求，受け取り，返却，複写をする際には登録利用者カードが必要となりますので，紛失したり破損したりしないでください。

A user card is required when using library terminals searching, requesting, receiving, returning and having materials photocopied; you should not lose or damage it.

図書館に持ち込めないもの
Items not to be brought into the Library

　以下の物品は館内への持ち込みが禁止されていますので，ロッカーに入れてください。ロッカーを利用するには 100 円硬貨を入れる必要があります。100 円硬貨は使用後に返却されます。傘は傘立てに入れてください。詳しくは国立国会図書館館内利用の手引きをご覧ください。

　　　　The Items listed in the box below are NOT allowed inside the Library. You are requested to put them in a locker. To use a locker, you need to put in a 100-yen coin. The coin will be returned when you open the locker again. Please put your umbrella in an umbrella stand. For the details, please see the Instructions for the On-site Use of the National Diet Library.

・7×10インチ(17×25cm)以上のバッグ，封筒，その他不透明な袋物，コピー機，カメラ，ビデオ，スキャナー，刃物，危険物，傘，その他図書館の財産を損傷したり他の利用者の迷惑になる可能性のあるもの。

　　　　・Bags, envelopes and any other opaque containers 7x10 inches (17x25cm) or larger, copiers, cameras, videos, scanners, blades, hazardous goods, umbrellas, and any other things that could damage library property or annoy other readers.

※　館内では携帯電話をマナーモードに設定し，通話は指定された場所でのみ行ってください。カメラ機能，録画・録音機能，ラジオ機能等の使用は禁止です。

※　パソコン，音の出る電卓などをお持ちの方は，図書館内の指定された場所でのみご使用ください。コンセントはご

利用いただけます。

* Please turn cell-phones to silent mode in the NDL building and speak on them only in the designated areas. Using the camera function, scanner and recording function, radio function, etc is prohibited.
* Visitors carrying a PC, sound-generating pocket calculator or other equipment must use it only in certain designated sections of the Library. Outlets are available.

退館　　**When leaving the NDL**

図書館を退館する際には，借りた資料をすべて返却してください。また，退館時にはカードを入口カウンターに返却してください（登録利用者カードは除く）。

Please return all the materials you have borrowed before you leave the Library. You must return the user card to the Entrance Counter when you leave the library (except Registration Cards).

忘れ物　　**Lost and found**

落とし物は図書館に保管されています。引き取るには，電話または下記までご連絡ください。

Lost property is kept in the Library. To reclaim, please call or visit:
Tel: 03-3581-2331, Lost and Found, NDL (1st floor, Main Building).

本項は「Quick Guide」(国立国会図書館)(https://www.ndl.go.jp/en/tokyo/flow/index.html)を加工して作成。

4. 国立国会図書館国際子ども図書館　利用案内

小さなお子様連れの方へ　　**For visitors with small children**

　ご来館には公共交通機関をご利用ください。JR 上野駅を使われる場合は，公園口が便利です。申し訳ありませんが，一般用駐車場はありませんので，自動車で来館される際は上野公園近隣の駐車場をご利用ください。

> To visit the International Library of Children's Literature (ILCL), please use public transport. If you use JR Ueno Station, the Park Gate is convenient.
>
> There is no parking for general use. Please use the parking near the Ueno Park when you visit by car.

おむつ替え等に利用できるベビーシート
Baby seat for changing diapers

　レンガ棟 1 階の「休憩・飲食・授乳スペース」やレンガ棟 1 階，3 階の多目的トイレには，おむつ替えに利用できるベビーシートがあります。

> There are baby seats that can be used for changing diapers in the Common Room and the multi-purpose toilets on the first and third floor of the Brick Building.

授乳スペース　　**Nursing space**

　レンガ棟 1 階の「休憩・飲食・授乳スペース」に，赤ちゃんへの授乳が必要な時に利用できるスペースがあります。また，ミルク用のお湯もご用意しています。

> There is a space that can be used when you need to breast-feed your baby in the Common Room. Hot water for bottled milk is also available.

食事スペース　　**Eating and drinking space**

　レンガ棟 1 階「カフェテリア」では，飲み物，軽食（サンドイッチ，スパゲティなど）などを提供しています。離乳食メニューなどはございません。

　持参されたお弁当などは，レンガ棟 1 階廊下の弁当席，「休憩・飲食・授乳スペース」または屋外テラスをご利用ください。

※　館内は指定場所を除き，飲食禁止となっております。ご協力をお願いします。

> Beverages and light meals (sandwiches, spaghetti, etc.) are available at the cafeteria on the first floor. There is no baby food.
>
> When you bring your lunch, please use tables and chairs for lunch in the corridor and the Common Room in the first floor of the Brick Building or the outdoor terrace. Please be considerate of others when using the tables and chairs.
>
> * Eating and drinking are prohibited in the library except in

the designated areas. Thank you for your cooperation.

トイレ　**Restrooms**

　レンガ棟 1 階・3 階，アーチ棟 1 階・2 階のトイレに子ども用便座を設置しています。また，手洗い場には 2 種類の高さを用意しました。

> There are toilet seats for children in the restrooms on the first and third floor of the Brick Building and on the first and second floor of the Arch Building. In addition, washstands with two levels are provided.

本項は「For visitors with small children」（国立国会図書館）（https://www.kodomo.go.jp/english/service/access/child.html）を加工して作成。

あとがき

　本書の旧版，『図書館員のための英会話ハンドブック　国内編』は 1996 年の刊行になります。以降，好評を博して数回の増刷を重ねていたものの，その後の社会状況の変化により，掲載内容が図書館現場に次第にそぐわない部分も見られてきました。旧版ではインターネットに関する記述は皆無であり，全体的に内容の古さが目立ってきましたが，類書が少ないこともあり，日本図書館協会のいわばロングセラーとなっていました。何回目かの増刷で在庫がゼロ近くなった時に，出版委員会で改訂版構想が持ち上がりました。10 年ほど前になります。旧版を踏まえながら，新たな状況を反映した文案を加えるという方向でスタートしましたが，旧来の文案を一部改訂する必要もあり，ペンディング状態になってしまいました。新たな執筆候補者探しも試みましたがなかなかご縁がなく，数年間，改訂作業が止まってしまいました。

　そこに 2021 年から出版委員会に参加された槇盛可那子氏が，改訂版作業への強力な推進役となり，今回の刊行の運びとなりました。旧版を最小限度の改訂にとどめる方針を維持したまま，既出のフレーズを追加・削除しながら，全体の統一性やコンセプトを崩さずに作業いただきました。また新しいイラストの必要性も考え，長谷川灯氏に依頼し，会話の理解を助けるイラスト 20 点以上を描いていただきました。ご多忙の中，イラスト作成をお引き受けくださった長谷川氏に感謝申し上げます。

旧版から今般の改訂版刊行までに 28 年経過しました。ここ
に至るまで多くの方にご協力・ご尽力をいただきました。旧版
著書の皆様には，改訂版刊行と著者表示等の許可をいただきま
した。日本図書館協会の出版委員会委員には，委員会での活発
な意見を頂戴しました。最後に，旧版と今回の改訂版の両方の
編集・製作を手掛けてくださった日本図書館協会事務局出版部
には，適時貴重なアドバイスをいただき，辛抱強く本書の脱稿
を見守ってくださいました。ここに厚くお礼申し上げます。

　本書にかかわってくださったすべての皆様に深く感謝申し上
げます。

　　　　　　　日本図書館協会出版委員会委員　　石井　保志

事項索引

【あ行】

ILL ネットワーク ･････････････････････ 81
ID カード ･････････････････････････････ 3, 30
宛名 ･･･････････････････････････････････ 132
アルファベット順 ･････････････････ 14, 17
医学図書館 ･･･････････････････････････ 99
傷みが激しい ･････････････････････････ 22
移動図書館 ･･･････････････････････ 47, 48
入口ホール ･･･････････････････････ 4, 19
印刷状態が悪い ･････････････････････ 133
インターネット ･･･････････ 104, 106, 117
ウェブサイト ･･････ 36, 40, 43, 70, 72, 83,
　88, 107, 110, 114, 117
受入れ ･･･････････････････････････ 57, 95
受付 ･･･････････････ 21, 39, 43, 49, 125
受付番号 ･････････････････････････････ 22
英字新聞 ･･････････････････････････････ 7
英文併記 ･････････････････････････････ 40
英訳 ･･･････････････････････････････････ 109
SNS ･･･････････････････････････････ 117, 118
SDI サービス ･･･････････････････････ 116
閲覧 ･･･････････ 19, 61, 62, 78, 90, 112
閲覧室 ･･･････････ 9, 10, 18, 19, 26, 57
エレベーター ･･･････････････････････ 32
延滞 ･･･････････ 59, 63, 66, 67, 76
延長 ･･･････････････ 43, 72, 73, 117

OPAC ･･･････････････ 9, 14, 15, 70, 91, 94,
　101, 102, 103, 105, 115, 117
おはなしのへや ･････････････････････ 8
おむつ替え ･･･････････････････････ 140
折りたたみの傘 ･･･････････････････ 30

【か行】

開架 ･･･････････････････････････ 7, 110
海外 ILL ･･･････････････････････････ 83
開架（式）書架 ･･･････････････ 17, 57
開館時間 ･･･････････････ 41, 42, 122
開館日 ･･･････････････････････････ 41
会議室 ･････････････････････････････ 8
開催 ･･･････････ 45, 117, 122, 125
回収 ･･･････････････････････････ 67
階段 ･･･････････････････････ 10, 32
回覧 ･･･････････････････････････ 18
夏期休暇期間 ･･･････････････ 43, 122
学位論文 ･･･････････････････････ 83
各種表示 ･･･････････････････････ 122
学生 ･･･････････ 2, 10, 25, 37, 93
学生証 ･･･････････ 3, 4, 11, 54
学童クラブ ･･･････････････････ 29
学部生 ･･･････････････････････ 59
火災報知器 ･･･････････････････ 33
火事 ･･･････････････････････････ 32

事項索引 ････････145

貸出 ……10, 11, 20, 27, 28, 29, 30, 37, 52, 54, 57, 58, 61, 63, 64, 72, 73, 78, 79, 90, 94, 110, 122, 124

貸出期間（期限）………58, 59, 65, 72

貸出規則…………………………57

貸出冊数…………………………58, 59

貸出中……………………………69, 94

貸出停止…………………………63, 67

貸出手続…………………………30

学会 ………45, 82, 107, 129

カード（クレジット）…………………22

カード（図書館利用）……3, 4, 13, 48, 53, 54, 55, 61, 63, 64, 66, 102

カード（入館）…………………………3

紙詰まり…………………………26

科目等履修生……………………54

館外貸出…………………30, 57, 58, 78

刊行 ………………………27, 106

刊行年月日………………………105

完全一致検索……………………104

巻頭………………………………105

館内閲覧…………………………61, 62

館内放送…………………………62, 124

巻末………………………………106

危険物……………………………138

期限を過ぎる……………59, 67, 76

寄稿………………………………119

貴重品……………………………5, 136

貴重本……………………………57

キャッシュレス決済……………22

キャビネット……………………19

キャンセル………………………13, 80

キャンパスマップ………………40

休館………………………41, 42, 43

教職員……………………………11, 25

許可………………………………83, 137

教務部……………………………55

拠点………………………………47

禁止事項…………………………123

禁帯出資料………………………57

グループ学習室…………………11

車の移動…………………………124, 125

クレジットカード………………22

クレーム処理………132, 133, 134

掲載巻号…………………………105

掲載ページ………………………105

軽食………………………………141

ゲーム……………………………118

研究員……………………………37

研究個室…………………………13

研究室……………………64, 90, 95

研究者……………………………119

研究所……………………………130, 131

研究費……………………………27

現金………………………22, 23, 75

言語の切替え……………………103

検索 ………43, 78, 97, 101, 103, 104, 110, 113, 114, 115, 117, 120, 137

検索結果…………………81, 102, 118

件名………………………………105

件名標目表………………………105

コイン式…………………………23, 64

公共図書館 ················ 37, 52, 109
工事 ······································ 44
講習会 ······························ 117, 125
更新 ·································· 43, 54
交通機関 ·························· 39, 140
交通系 IC カード ···················· 22
購読 ············ 81, 88, 119, 132, 133, 134
購入 ············ 7, 23, 26, 27, 28, 83
購入依頼（希望）·············· 27, 28
高齢者施設 ························· 29
国立国会図書館 ········· 108, 110, 111,
　112, 115, 135, 136, 138, 140
五十音順 ··························· 17
小銭 ································· 23
コピーカード式 ····················· 23
コピー機 ············ 23, 26, 64, 138
混配 ································· 17

【さ行】

在学，在勤 ························· 37
在住 ································· 37
最新号 ·························· 57, 88, 95
最新版 ······························ 88
再発行 ······························ 56
在留カード ······················ 52, 53
索引 ································· 134
雑誌 ············ 7, 8, 10, 14, 16, 17, 18, 27,
　57, 58, 81, 83, 93, 95, 108, 115, 119,
　129, 130, 131, 132, 133, 134, 135
雑誌室 ······························ 17
冊子体 ······························ 115

雑誌名 ········ 105, 106, 114, 124, 134
雑誌論文 ··························· 81
参考図書 ··························· 57
参考図書室 ························· 10
参照 ································· 132
至急 ············ 76, 124, 125, 132, 133
事項調査 ··························· 97
辞書 ·································· 15, 57
地震 ································· 32
システム更新 ······················ 43
施設案内 ···························· 7
施設の利用・予約 ················· 11
視聴覚室 ······················· 5, 91, 92
実費 ································· 80
CD ·································· 58, 91
CD-ROM ···························· 106
自動貸出機 ························· 64
児童書 ······························ 7
自動書庫 ··························· 15
自動販売機 ························· 23
品切れ ······························ 74
支払 ···················· 25, 26, 75, 80
絞り込み ························· 102, 104
事務室（所）·················· 26, 94, 131
社員証 ······························ 53
写真撮影 ··························· 118
住所 ········ 47, 52, 53, 129, 130, 131,
　132, 134
収書方針 ··························· 28
修理 ································· 26, 60
祝祭日 ······························ 42

縮刷版 …………………………… 19
主題 …………… 74, 86, 91, 99, 119
出庫依頼票 ……………………… 15
出版 ……………… 95, 104, 129, 130
出版社 …………………… 83, 104
出版物 …………………… 128, 132
取得価格 ………………………… 75
授乳 …………………… 140, 141
受領 …………………… 130, 132
受領書 …………………… 129, 130
巡回 …………………… 47, 48
上映会 …………………………… 122
障害者サービス ……………… 29
紹介状 …………………… 2, 38
詳細表示 ………………………… 102
小説 …………………… 86, 109
使用中 …………………… 12, 69
省略 …………………………… 106
書架 ………… 14, 16, 17, 20, 23, 32,
57, 69, 73, 91, 93, 94, 95, 100, 102
書架番号 ………………………… 16
食堂 …………………… 8, 32
所在調査 ………………………… 93
書誌 …………………… 105, 106
所蔵 …… 16, 19, 23, 24, 28, 87, 88, 90, 95
所蔵事項 ………………………… 16
所蔵情報 ………………………… 102
庶務課 …………………………… 27
書名 …… 14, 66, 89, 99, 103, 104, 124
新館 …………………… 135, 136, 137
新着雑誌 …………………… 17, 18

新聞 …………… 7, 8, 14, 18, 19
新聞閲覧室 ……………………… 10
新聞閲覧台 ……………………… 19
推薦状 …………………………… 38
スペル …………………… 49, 89, 104
スマートフォン ……………… 30
請求 …………………… 43, 80, 137
請求記号 …… 14, 15, 16, 28, 61, 90, 91,
102
請求書 …………………………… 132
政府刊行物 ……………………… 108
製本雑誌 …………………… 17, 18
整理中 …………………………… 70
政令指定都市立図書館 ……… 78, 110
絶版 …………………… 28, 74
セミナールーム ………………… 117
セルフコピー機 ………………… 23
専門図書館 ……………………… 37
専門分野 ………………………… 130
専用端末 …………………… 13, 117
相互貸借 ………………………… 77
操作 …………………………… 25
蔵書 …………… 47, 57, 78, 101
蔵書数 …………………………… 7
蔵書点検 …………………… 42, 122
送付 ……… 81, 130, 131, 133, 134
送料 …………………………… 111
卒業証明書 ……………………… 55
卒業生 …………………………… 54

【た行】

大学院生 ……………………………… 59
大学図書館 …………… 54, 114, 115, 128
大活字本 ……………………………… 29
退館 …………………………… 30, 139
台風 …………………………………… 43
代理店 ……………………………… 133
宅配サービス ………………………… 29
タブレット ………………… 10, 11, 30
単行本 ……………… 8, 14, 58, 99, 132
団体貸出 ……………………………… 29
団体情報 …………………………… 107
端末 ………… 9, 13, 19, 70, 78, 112,
　113, 117, 137
地域住民 ……………………………… 54
地域資料室 ………………………… 8, 20
地下 ………………………… 8, 73, 122
近くの図書館 ……………………… 110
地下書庫 ……………………… 18, 102
逐次刊行物 ………………………… 16, 64
中学校 ………………………………… 88
駐車場 ……………………………… 140
調査 …………… 86, 93, 97, 98, 119
著作権法 ……………………………… 21
著者 ………… 83, 89, 99, 103, 104, 105,
　128, 134
通学先・勤務先 ……………………… 53
DAISY ………………………………… 29
提示する ……………………………… 3, 6
テキスト化 …………………………… 29
手数料 ……………………………… 56, 80

データベース ………… 81, 97, 112.113,
　114, 117, 125
手続き ……… 2, 3, 11, 13, 52, 61, 63, 72,
　117
手荷物 ………………………………… 6
電源 ………………………………… 10
電光掲示板 …………………………… 15
展示 ………………… 10, 18, 27, 122
電子化 ……………………………… 29
電子ジャーナル ……… 112, 113, 114, 116
点字図書 ……………………………… 29
添付 ………………………………… 132
電話番号 ……………………………… 53
トイレ …………………… 8, 10, 140, 142
統計 ……………………………… 108
統計資料室 ………………………… 109
投稿 ……………………………… 119
投稿規定 …………………………… 119
登録 ……………… 52, 53, 54, 116, 136
督促 ………………………………… 76
特別永住者証明書 ………………… 52, 53
特別警報 ……………………………… 43
図書カウンター …………………… 124
図書館見学 ………………………… 3, 45
特許情報 ……………………… 119, 120
都道府県立図書館 ………………… 78, 110
取消し ………………………………… 71
取引書店 ……………………………… 27
取り寄せ …… 16, 68, 78, 79, 80, 81, 83,
　90, 111

事項索引 ……… 149

【な行】

内線 ……………………………… 87, 96

日本関係欧文図書目録 ……………105

日本十進分類法（NDC）……… 14, 99,
　100, 101

荷物 …………………………… 4, 5, 6

入館 …………………2, 3, 4, 135, 136, 137

入手 ………………… 79, 81, 82, 83

入力 ………………………… 101, 118

布の絵本 …………………………… 29

年中無休 …………………………… 42

年度始め …………………………… 54

【は行】

配架 ………………… 8, 14, 17, 18, 69, 91

配送 ………………………………… 29

配列 ………………………………106

バーコード ………………………… 64

バーコード決済 …………………… 22

破損 ………………………………137

バックナンバー ………… 17, 86, 130

発行 ………………… 4, 53, 54, 55, 130

発送 ………………………… 80, 133

罰則 ………………………………… 59

刃物 ………………………………138

春休み……………………………… 59

番号順……………………………… 15

筆記用具…………………………… 5

必要事項…………………………… 69

避難 ………………………………… 32

ビニール袋 ……………………… 5, 6

百科事典 …………………………… 15

費用 ………………… 24, 79, 82, 83

表示 ………… 15, 65, 102, 103, 115, 122

複写 ………… 10, 21, 23, 24, 25, 43, 83,
　124, 134, 137

複写禁止 …………………………… 22

蓋つきの飲み物 …………………… 9

負担する………………… 60, 80, 111

ブックポスト ……………………… 67

ブラウザ …………………………115

プリントアウト …………………115

フロアマップ ……………………… 11

プロジェクター …………………… 11

プルダウン ………………………101

フルテキスト ……………………115

文献 ………… 81, 97, 100, 102, 105, 106,
　108, 112

文献複写 …………………………134

紛失 …………………55, 74, 123, 137

分類 ………… 14, 99, 100, 106, 120

分類体系 …………………………… 99

分類番号 …………………………100

分類法（表）…………………… 99, 100

閉架書庫 …………… 7, 17, 19, 61

閉館 ………………… 41, 42, 122

閉館の時間 ………………………124

別館 …………………………… 9, 10

別置する ……………………………15

ヘルプ機能 ………………………103

返却 ………… 3, 5, 56, 59, 62, 63, 66, 67,
　68, 69, 70, 73, 76, 94, 123, 124, 137,

138, 139

返却（用）カート ……………… 69, 94

返却期限 ………… 63, 66, 76, 122

変更する ………………… 115, 122

弁償する ……………… 60, 74, 75

返送料 ………………………… 80

弁当 …………………………… 141

保育園 ………………………… 29

法令資料室 ………………… 10, 16

保管する ……………… 19, 122, 139

ホワイトボード ………………… 11

本館 ……………… 10, 90, 135, 137

本の読み聞かせ ………………… 9

【ま行】

マイクロフィッシュ …………… 19

マイクロフィルム ………… 19, 25

マイクロフィルムリーダー ……… 25

迷子 …………………………… 125

又貸し ………………………… 123

待ち時間 ……………………… 21

丸 1 日 ………………………… 12

ミスコピー …………………… 134

未製本雑誌 …………………… 18

未製本棚 ……………………… 18

身分証明書 ……………… 3, 4, 55

無効なカード …………………… 4

無断 ……………… 31, 95, 124

無料 …………………… 54, 122

無料の Wi-Fi …………………… 10

迷惑 …………………… 123, 138

申し込み ………… 11, 12, 13, 15, 16, 21,
27, 61, 78, 92, 117

申込用紙 ……………………… 80

目録 ……………… 20, 90, 110

催し物案内 …………………… 122

最寄りの駅 …………………… 39

【や行】

薬学図書館 …………………… 45

有効期限 ……………………… 55

郵送料 ………………………… 81

USB …………………………… 118

用紙に記入 ……… 2, 12, 53, 61, 80, 92

予約 ……… 11, 12, 13, 43, 69, 70, 71, 72,
76, 102, 117, 125

予約表 ………………………… 12

予約申込書 ………………… 69, 70

【ら行】

来館 ……………… 29, 38, 140

落丁 …………………………… 133

ラーニングコモンズ …………… 11

乱丁 …………………………… 133

リクエストサービス ………… 26, 78

リザーブ・カウンター ………… 73

離乳食 ………………………… 141

利用案内 ………… 11, 99, 135, 140

両替機 ………………………… 23

料金 ……… 21, 22, 81, 82, 137

利用資格 ………………… 27, 37

利用者 ……… 2, 3, 57, 113, 123, 135,

事項索引 ……… 151

136, 138, 139

利用者登録 ……………… 135, 136, 137

臨時休館 ……………………………… 43

隣接市 ………………………………… 37

礼状 ……………………………… 129, 130

レシート ……………………………… 65

レファレンスカウンター ……… 8, 20

レファレンスサービス …………… 85

レファレンス担当者 ……… 28, 86, 113

レファレンスデスク ……………… 113

レファレンスブック …………… 8, 105

連絡先 …………………… 71, 98, 107

連絡通路 ……………………… 9, 135

ログイン ………………… 70, 72, 118

論題 ……………………………… 105

論文 ………… 24, 82, 83, 112, 114,
115, 116, 134

【わ行】

忘れ物 ………………… 49, 122, 124, 139

■執筆者・編者紹介

◆初版　執筆者（ABC 順，所属は執筆当時）

古林　洽子（ふるばやし　ひろこ）　中外製薬㈱中央研究所図書室

松本　和子（まつもと　かずこ）　慶應義塾大学湘南藤沢メディアセンター

高田　宜美（たかだ　よしみ）　㈶国際医学情報センター

田中理恵子（たなか　りえこ）　目黒区立守屋図書館

John A. Tokarz（ジョン・A. トカーズ）　上智大学比較文化学部助教授

塚田　洋（つかだ　ひろし）　国立国会図書館

◆改訂版　編者（ABC 順，◎は委員長，○は主担当）

出版委員会

　原　　修（はら　おさむ）　立教学院

◎長谷川豊祐（はせがわ　とよひろ）　図書館笑顔プロジェクト

　畠山　珠美（はたけやま　たまみ）　前・国際基督教大学

　樋渡えみ子（ひわたり　えみこ）　元・東京都立図書館

○石井　保志（いしい　やすし）　元・東京医科歯科大学図書館（現・東京科学大学）

○槇盛可那子（まきもり　かなこ）　東京都立中央図書館

　蓑田　明子（みのだ　あきこ）　東大和市子ども家庭支援センター

　小田　光宏（おだ　みつひろ）　青山学院大学

　大谷　康晴（おおたに　やすはる）　青山学院大学

　鈴木　宏宗（すずき　ひろむね）　国立国会図書館

　立石亜紀子（たていし　あきこ）　お茶の水女子大学附属図書館

◆本文イラスト

長谷川　灯（はせがわ　とも）

◆JLA 図書館実践シリーズ　48

**図書館員のための英会話ハンドブック
国内編　改訂版**

1996 年 9 月 5 日　　初版第 1 刷発行©
2024 年11月20日　　改訂版第 1 刷発行
2025 年 3 月20日　　改訂版第 2 刷発行

定価：本体 1700円（税別）

編　者：日本図書館協会出版委員会
発行者：公益社団法人　日本図書館協会
　　　　〒104-0033　東京都中央区新川1-11-14
　　　　Tel 03-3523-0811㈹　Fax 03-3523-0841
デザイン：笠井亞子
印刷所：㈱丸井工文社
Printed in Japan
JLA202438　　ISBN978-4-8204-2408-6
本文の用紙は中性紙を使用しています。

JLA 図書館実践シリーズ　刊行にあたって

　日本図書館協会出版委員会が「図書館員選書」を企画して 20 年あまりが経過した。図書館学研究の入門と図書館現場での実践の手引きとして，図書館関係者の座右の書を目指して刊行されてきた。

　しかし，新世紀を迎え数年を経た現在，本格的な情報化社会の到来をはじめとして，大きく社会が変化するとともに，図書館に求められるサービスも新たな展開を必要としている。市民の求める新たな要求に対応していくために，従来の枠に納まらない新たな理論構築と，先進的な図書館の実践成果を踏まえた，利用者と図書館員のための出版物が待たれている。

　そこで，新シリーズとして，「JLA 図書館実践シリーズ」をスタートさせることとなった。図書館の発展と変化する時代に即応しつつ，図書館をより一層市民のものとしていくためのシリーズ企画であり，図書館にかかわり意欲的に研究，実践を積み重ねている人々の力が出版事業に生かされることを望みたい。

　また，新世紀の図書館学への導入の書として，一般利用者の図書館利用に資する書として，図書館員の仕事の創意や疑問に答えうる書として，図書館にかかわる内外の人々に支持されていくことを切望するものである。

2004 年 7 月 20 日

日本図書館協会出版委員会

委員長　松島　茂

図書館員と図書館を知りたい人たちのための新シリーズ！
JLA 図書館実践シリーズ 既刊40冊，好評発売中

（価格は本体価格）

1. **実践型レファレンスサービス入門　補訂2版**
   斎藤文男・藤村せつ子著／203p／1800円

2. **多文化サービス入門**
   日本図書館協会多文化サービス研究委員会／198p／1800円

3. **図書館のための個人情報保護ガイドブック**
   藤倉恵一著／149p／1600円

4. **公共図書館サービス・運動の歴史1**　そのルーツから戦後にかけて
   小川徹ほか著／266p／2100円

5. **公共図書館サービス・運動の歴史2**　戦後の出発から現代まで
   小川徹ほか著／275p／2000円

6. **公共図書館員のための消費者健康情報提供ガイド**
   ケニヨン・カシーニ著／野添篤毅監訳／262p／2000円

7. **インターネットで文献探索　2022年版**
   伊藤民雄著／207p／1800円

8. **図書館を育てた人々　イギリス篇**
   藤野幸雄・藤野寛之著／304p／2000円

9. **公共図書館の自己評価入門**
   神奈川県図書館協会図書館評価特別委員会編／152p／1600円

10. **図書館長の仕事**　「本のある広場」をつくった図書館長の実践記
    ちばおさむ著／172p／1900円

11. **手づくり紙芝居講座**
    ときわひろみ著／194p／1900円

12. **図書館と法**　図書館の諸問題への法的アプローチ　改訂版増補
    鑓水三千男著／354p／2000円

13. **よい図書館施設をつくる**
    植松貞夫ほか著／125p／1800円

14. **情報リテラシー教育の実践**　すべての図書館で利用教育を
    日本図書館協会図書館利用教育委員会編／180p／1800円

15. **図書館の歩む道**　ランガナタン博士の五法則に学ぶ
    竹内悊解説／295p／2000円

16. **図書分類からながめる本の世界**
    近江哲史著／201p／1800円

17. **闘病記文庫入門**　医療情報資源としての闘病記の提供方法
    石井保志著／212p／1800円

18. **児童図書館サービス1**　運営・サービス論
    日本図書館協会児童青少年委員会児童図書館サービス編集委員会編／310p／1900円

19. **児童図書館サービス2**　児童資料・資料組織論
    日本図書館協会児童青少年委員会児童図書館サービス編集委員会編／322p／1900円

20. **「図書館学の五法則」をめぐる188の視点**　『図書館の歩む道』読書会から
    竹内悊編／160p／1700円

図書館員と図書館を知りたい人たちのための新シリーズ！
JLA図書館実践シリーズ 既刊40冊，好評発売中

21. 新着雑誌記事速報から始めてみよう　RSS・APIを活用した図書館サービス
牧野雄二・川嶋斉著／161p／1600円

22. 図書館員のためのプログラミング講座
山本哲也著／160p／1600円

23. RDA入門　目録規則の新たな展開
上田修一・蟹瀬智弘著／205p／1800円

24. 図書館史の書き方，学び方　図書館の現在と明日を考えるために
奥泉和久著／246p／1900円

25. 図書館多読への招待
酒井邦秀・西澤一編著／186p／1600円

26. 障害者サービスと著作権法　第2版
日本図書館協会障害者サービス委員会，著作権委員会編／151p／1600円

27. 図書館資料としてのマイクロフィルム入門
小島浩之編／180p／1700円

28. 法情報の調べ方入門　法の森のみちしるべ　第2版
ロー・ライブラリアン研究会編／221p／1800円

29. 東松島市図書館 3.11からの復興　東日本大震災と向き合う
加藤孔敬著／270p／1800円

30. 「図書館のめざすもの」を語る
第101回全国図書館大会第14分科会運営委員編／151p／1500円

31. 学校図書館の教育力を活かす　学校を変える可能性
塩見昇著／178p／1600円

32. NDCの手引き　「日本十進分類法」新訂10版入門
小林康隆編著，日本図書館協会分類委員会監修／208p／1600円

33. サインはもっと自由につくる　人と棚とをつなげるツール
中川卓美著／177p／1600円

34. 〈本の世界〉の見せ方　明定流コレクション形成論
明定義人著／142p／1500円

35. はじめての電子ジャーナル管理　改訂版
保坂睦著／250p／1800円

36. パッと見てピン！ 動作観察で利用者支援　理学療法士による20の提案
結城俊也著／183p／1700円

37. 図書館利用に障害のある人々へのサービス 上巻　利用者・資料・サービス編　補訂版
日本図書館協会障害者サービス委員会編／304p／1800円

38. 図書館利用に障害のある人々へのサービス 下巻　先進事例・制度・法規編　補訂版
日本図書館協会障害者サービス委員会編／320p／1800円

39. 図書館とゲーム　イベントから収集へ
井上奈智・高倉暁大・日向良和著／170p／1600円

40. 図書館多読のすすめかた
西澤一・米澤久美子・粟野真紀子編著／198p／1700円